Thomas Gordon Hake

Madeline

With Other Poems and Parables

Thomas Gordon Hake

Madeline
With Other Poems and Parables

ISBN/EAN: 9783744760867

Printed in Europe, USA, Canada, Australia, Japan

Cover: Foto ©Thomas Meinert / pixelio.de

More available books at **www.hansebooks.com**

MADELINE

WITH

OTHER POEMS AND PARABLES.

BY

THOMAS GORDON HAKE, *M.D.*

LONDON:
CHAPMAN AND HALL, 193, PICCADILLY.
1871.

CONTENTS.

MADELINE.

	PAGE
PROLOGUE	1
PART I.	13
,, II.	19
,, III.	29
,, IV.	35
,, V.	38
,, VI.	44
,, VII.	51
,, VIII.	59
,, IX.	66
,, X.	71
,, XI.	77
,, XII.	83
,, XIII.	99
,, XIV.	109
EPILOGUE	117

TALES.

THE LILY OF THE VALLEY	127
THE DEADLY NIGHTSHADE	140
IMMORTALITY	149
OLD SOULS	157

THE WORLD'S EPITAPH.

		PAGE
Epitaph	I. On Art	169
,,	II. On Music	171
,,	III. On Poetry	172
,,	IV. On the Storm of Life	173
,,	V. On the Rainbow	175
	Epode	176
,,	VI. On the Sanctuary	177
	Epode	180
,,	VII. On Nature	181
,,	VIII. On Time	183
,,	IX. On the Future	184
,,	X. On the Soul	186
,,	XI. On the Soul	187
	Epode	188
,,	XII. On Glory	189
,,	XIII. On Peace	190
,,	XIV. On the Valley of the Shadow	191
	Epode	192
,,	XV. On Genius	193
	Epode	195
,,	XVI. On Departing Peace	196
,,	XVII. On Nature	197
,,	XVIII. On Life	198
,,	XIX. On Hope	199
,,	XX. On Thought	200
	Epode	201
,,	XXI. On the Seasons of Life	202
	Epode	204
,,	XXII. On Passion	205
	Epode	207

Contents.

		PAGE
EPITAPH XXIII. ON THE NUPTIALS	. . . .	208
EPODE	. . . .	209
„ XXIV. ON THE SIREN	. . . .	210
„ XXV. ON THE IMAGE	. . . .	212
EPODE	. . . .	213
„ XXVI. ON THE INFANT AT THE BREAST	.	214
„ XXVII. ON THE WIDOW	. . . .	215
EPODE	. . . .	216
„ XXVIII. ON PITY	. . . .	217
„ XXIX. ON THE BEREAVED	. . .	218
EPODE	. . . .	222
„ XXX. ON EARLY DEATH	. . .	223
EPODE	. . . .	224
„ XXXI. ON THE DESERTED	. . .	225
„ XXXII. ON DISSIPATED YOUTH	. . .	227
EPODE	. . . .	228
„ XXXIII. ON CONSCIENCE	. . . .	229
„ XXXIV. ON SLUMBER	. . . .	230
„ XXXV. ON THE PILLOW OF THE WRETCHED		231
EPODE	. . . .	231
„ XXXVI. ON A MOTHER	. . .	233
EPODE	. . . .	234
EPODE	. . .	235
„ XXXVII. ON THE OUTCAST	. . . .	236
EPODE	. . . .	238
„ XXXVIII. ON CHARITY	. . . .	239
EPODE	. . .	240
„ XXXIX. ON THE SAINT	. . . .	241
EPODE	. . . .	242
„ XL. ON THE SISTER OF MERCY	. .	243

Contents.

			PAGE
Epitaph	XLI.	On the Statesman	244
		Epode	245
,,	XLII.	On Old Age	246
		Epode	246
,,	XLIII.	On Penitence	247
,,	XLIV.	On Madness	250
,,	XLV.	On Despair	252
,,	XLVI.	On the Struggle for Immortality	253
		Epode	253
,,	XLVII.	On Man	254
,,	XLVIII.	On Fate	256
,,	XLIX.	On Despotism	258
,,	L.	On Pride	259
,,	LI.	On the Prisoner	261
,,	LII.	On Remorse	262
,,	LIII.	On Hypocrisy	264
		Epode	265
,,	LIV.	On the Mask	266
,,	LV.	On Self-Righteousness	267
,,	LVI.	On Cunning	268
,,	LVII.	On Belief	269
		Epode	270
,,	LVIII.	On the Death-bed of the Wise	271
,,	LIX.	On the Philosopher	273
,,	LX.	On Delirium	274
,,	LXI.	On the Close of Life	276
		Epode	277
,,	LXII.	On the Chuchyard	278
,,	LXIII.	On the Tombs	280
,,	LXIV.	On Death	281
,,	LXV.	On the Resurgam	283

MADELINE.

MADELINE.

PROLOGUE.

VALCLUSA.

A TWILIGHT breaks in tints of sober gray
Between the last of night and first of day:
The pallid dusk a straggling horror brings
On ebbing rush of midnight's ruffled wings.
In Nature's absence, by what hand is cleft
This sleep asunder and this terror left?
Our eyes, confused, we all at once unclose,
To find each other severed from repose.
What miss we wildly staring out of sleep
While towards the dreamy side our senses keep?

The not long barren sky, like spring-time, flowers;
Its red and aureate bloom a perfume showers
To mollify the scent of curdled gore,
That what has been may seem to be no more.
But no thin sorcery, skimmed off stagnant breath
That fathoms deep lies gathered over death,
Can put a deed aside and clear the track,
Or drive the ghost-like memory of it back.
Though silence bind the vale, the shining dews
Have cleansed the sky and dropped the chilling news
On silvery cobwebs, o'er the meadows spun
To catch the fire-flies hatched upon the sun.
The while we slept beneath the sorcerer's spell
A deed was done that waked a wish in hell,
A deed was done that startled paradise:
Nor hell nor heaven recovers its surprise.
The fresh done deed begins to canker time,
Then be it fixed in some symbolic rhyme
Ere yet too late, the traces too far spent
To dedicate a song to its lament.

Sweet as the pipe's, loud as the clarion's blast,
There is a voice, heard oftenest in the past;
It warbles like a nightingale's whose thrill
Shakes as a reed the honey-gurgler's bill,
And sets the foliage rustling as it rings,
While every bush has turned its leaves to wings:

The voice of Nature, never wholly spent!
Shall we invoke its notes for our lament?
Then throat to throat shall songsters rend the grove
And share with us the trouble and the love;
Consenting rhymes shall touch the brink of bliss,
And end each fairy couplet with a kiss.
Ours be the rapture while to them belong
The willing tones of this enchanted song,
That so to distant streams the news disperse
While culminates in love the modest verse.
Or will the sickened Muse heaven's panpipe stop
And in oblivion's mist the memory drop?

CHORUS OF NYMPHS.

That voice, once heard, is mute,
And stringless is the lute.
The chords no more the note of love prolong
   That swept the cadent rhyme,
And twice bemoaned a wrong:
   In pity and in chime.
Lost too the choral lay
Whose music once gave solace to the day.
· Spirits no longer crowd the air
That wistful bent, with finger on the lip,
   Sad thoughts to sip;
   To cull the softer tones of harsh despair.

VALCLUSA.

A fearless sun rips up a crimson cloud,
Of deeds fresh done in night the loosened shroud.
He runs his course, too busy on his way
To tell a tale of deeds not done in day,
Or should he glare upon the hardening clot
He plunges on, the secret heeding not.
Though now man's blood attaints the breath of space
Soon shall its fine evincement leave no trace:
Be it assized, then, ere its aspect pale
To match the simpler colours of the vale.
Let us the heaving cause of conscience plead,
Till the grand key-note sounded takes the lead;
The chorus lift till all the earth repeat
To music's heart the palpitating beat.
Let us evoke the souls whose bodies stay
To yet identify the suffering clay,
Recal the voice that quivers like a tear
Unable all its heaviness to bear,
Recal the sobs all troubled as they fall;
Fragments of love, all feeling pain for all.

CHORUS.

What hand arrests the fire
That lingers in the lyre?

The nuptial strain of love and music wed
    Was rapture to the ear;
The fierce desires it fed
    To smite them with a tear.
Who now partakes the spell?
Whom once it moved in sleepy marble dwell.
    A ripple dreams upon the rill
Beside the Muses' tomb and murmurs not
Of joys forgot,
    But to the dead imparts a deeper chill.

Cold is the hand that smote
The once melodious note
Whose themes, the pride and glory of the past,
    Yet stir the fount of love:
The words that ever last
    In song immortal wove.
O deep-toned Sympathy!
Where is the heart that cares for woman's cry?
    A pity came from heaven of yore,
When suppliant maid for safe asylum trod
The floor of God,
    But now her hapless lot shall none deplore!

VALCLUSA.

Be it our part, sweet nymphs, through second sight,
To drag the deeds, now over, back to light.
Let me declare the theme, while all around
The hymn prolong, for this is hallowed ground.
Here Sorga's stream is sacred as of old,
Loved by the Muses: here the tale be told.
But let us first to them address the vow:
If they assist us smooth the verse shall flow,
Should they impede us wayward must it stray,
And gurgle wildly on its wavy way.

CHORUS.

O ye who once redressed
The wrongs of the distressed;
Turned into pity by the crystal tear,
   Attune this verse to song!
A sister's troubles hear,
   Ye who to heaven belong!
And may the anthem swell
With deeper woe than that vexed child befel!
   To terror may the strain arise,
The warblings blended with her lover's cry
As death sweeps by
   To claim him for the final sacrifice!

The nymphs of Sorga sing :
To heaven their voices cling.
Up to the Giver of all poesy
  Higher and higher wends
The message through the sky,
  And Heaven the answer sends!
Who drink of Sorga's wave,
Shall not in vain divine assistance crave.
  As eventide comes quickly on,
The shade of sleep is followed by a beam,
The shade of dream;
  And Sorga's brook ascends to Helicon!

Sorga, O seat of Love!
The softest airs that rove
The soul, with thee are set in unison;
  But now by rustling waves
That soul is hurried on ;
  A melody that raves
Is mingled in its thrill,
Not at the heart love's promise to fulfil.
  Thou noted brook that here abid'st,
A rapture at thy brink thou waftest high,
With frequent sigh,
  And to the heavens thy lowly lot confid'st!

VALCLUSA.

Behold the ether opens clear and wide;
The mountain is before us in its pride.
Above the pendant stream which glistens still,
A torrent swells, now rushes o'er the rill;
Another spouts, it tracks the frothy way,
To whence it fell returning back the spray.
The joining waters through the forest dash,
Torrents on torrents on the valley flash,
Reclaim the dried-up gorge where pine and rock
Lie under sentence of an earthquake's shock.
Wedged in by stones and trees in mingled heaps,
One billow eddies and another leaps;
One scoops the delf, another sweeps the wood,
And bears all onward; every wave a flood:
A cascade now, and now a foaming spire,
More fierce than flame these conquerors of fire.
O glorious emblems sent us to display
The human passions on their thoughtless way;
Bent now on conquest, now with victory flushed,
Now smooth as death—as motionless, as hushed.
Yes, this is Nature, proudly as she chafes:
The sign to her beloved the Muse vouchsafes.
Heard is the prayer, deep-toned; the answer felt;
Sent by the good before whose house we knelt.

Step forth, ungentle form,
Who shak'st the unwieldy storm!
Evoke thy actors marshalled to pursue
   Too far the lethal torch;
Its failing flame to rue
   At the sepulchral porch.
Tread thou the troubled stage
To move remorse, not anguish to assuage!
   Graceless behind the scenes appear
The mask, the timbrel, the wild fantasies
Of wicked eyes.
   Is she divine who honours not the tear?

Shall her loose smile prevail,
And none the lost bewail?
The woven thread of woe asunder snapped,
   Her hands above her head
Like silent cymbals clapped
   To speed the youthful dead!
Shall slowly melting sorrow
Be hustled into newly risen morrow?
   Yet now the thong would one unlash,
Let go the heart fresh leaping from its seat
To freedom's beat;
   The soughing wind drowned in the timbrel's crash.

CHORUS.

Is now not heard a chaunt
Within the sacred haunt?
A faltering echo falls into the plain
   To sweeten life below:
The Muses wake again
   In its return and flow!
But why among the Nine
Takes Comedy the lead in life divine?
   Seen is her quaint and smiling face,
While, as of old, her genial look extends
O'er all that ends,
   To cheer the world with its bewitching grace.

The grieving, absent gaze
When lost in dreamy maze,
She measures with the meaning of her eyes.
   If with the tear she pleads,
The smile upon it lies.
   All joy in heaven she leads!
She mimics human rage
With cheeks that burn and shrivel up to age,
   While yet the holy laughter rings.
And when with sorrow and its kindred ills
Her mould she fills,
   About the cast her gladsome spirit clings.

Her tones an echo start
Within the silent heart.
The gnawing worm the warder of that cell
  Beneath her look recoils;
And, stiffening in the spell,
  Ends its eternal toils.
She throws up souls at play,
And wins them life for yet another day!
  She lights on truth as by surprise.
What tongue-tied Nature artfully conceals
Her laugh reveals:
  Mirth for the simple, wisdom for the wise.

No cloud with fleecy rim
Her face serene can dim,
Nor give her brow a transitory shade.
  Nor, save in mockery,
Can fear that face invade,
  Or sadness dull that eye.
Prophetic is her gaze;
No portents sent as omens, her amaze.
  She takes the choice of loss and gain!
Let human love be offered up to vice
In sacrifice,
  She snatches pleasure from the bed of pain.

To the seduced who grieve
Their error to retrieve,
Yet sink in sin and sorrow till they die,
   She knows the magic art,
Not Nature to deny,
   But rapture to impart.
The deeper set the wrong,
The nobler glow the thoughts that round it throng.
   The ills of life she reconciles,
In scornful words that tragedy transcend,
Yet oddly blend
   In the infection of her dubious smiles.

All ending well at last,
Into her net is cast.
She tangles rage within the lyric strain:
   To some she gives the song,
To some the soft refrain
   Its burden to prolong.
They hymn the sister's fate;
The love-worn tale of terror they relate:
   They act the parts, to Nature true,
Till sunset gathers and expiring day
Breathes its last ray,
   This dream investing in its sombre hue.

I.

VALCLUSA.

Were they the shadeless figures of a dream
By fancy lighted at the silver beam?
A broken moon bends over us asleep;
One half above, one sunken in the deep.
Or were they shadows of the golden ray
That graced our eyes at last decline of day?
Yet as the leaf and flower our vision stain
And, once beheld, for evermore remain,
So has this tale our senses overgrown,
To be like Nature evermore our own.
A maid too fair to own a better fate,
Her thirst of love quenched in pernicious hate;
At eve seduced, upon the morrow roused
To maiden shame amid the disespoused;
Was Madeline, whom all spirits glorify
Above the vestals who unblemished die.

This end achieved by him whose hidden arts
A jealous power to intellect imparts:
A sage who watched for Nature's fickle mood
To bend her adverse attitude to good.
But who of Hermes oft has not heard tell,
The sorcerer whom this partial lot befel?
He knew all spirits, nymphs who still frequent
These streams whose mainspring is the firmament,
Or who, translated to another sphere,
Still their lost world to ecstasy revere.
One, Daphne named, he loved; on one same field
Pale-wise their hearts were set as in a shield.
Her birth, eventful deemed by loving eyes
That looked upon it through the anxious skies;
Her sudden flight, called up lest heart so fond
So soon to love should reach the pang beyond;
All this, euphonious metre let express,
And mortal ears with thoughts of her address.
Let us recal, though little time below
She stayed her first affections to bestow,
Let us recal to life her happy face,
That seemed with heaven for ever changing place!

CHORUS.

This is the vale whose name,
Dear to the lists of fame,

Valclusa bears; the secrets locked in sleep
  Are here divulged to all:
How some in slumber weep
  Though ills may not befal;
How some by dreams are bent
On anger adverse to their soul's intent.
How some with eyes fast shut converse;
  How some with every sense but one confin'd
Within the mind,
  Their lily hands in human gore immerse.

VALCLUSA.

Within this happy vale
Is Sorga's bed—the tale
Valclusa tells, herself a happy bride;
  Her time one joyous day,
  She lingers by its side
  And whiles her life away.
Now hear Valclusa's dream:
It shall light up the banks of Sorga's stream.
  Queen of the Nymphs whose fadeless charms
Bathe in the spring that sparkles through her fields,
She rapture yields
  In sweet embrace to Sorga's constant arms.

Rocks that the blood congeal
The river-god conceal.

He rushes forth enamoured of her grove.
  In eddying light he glides,
And ever with his love
  In ecstasy abides.
Nymphs thence their days begin
And life, not mortal, from her bosom win.
  Behold in every leaping beam
That sucks the wave, a spark of life has clomb
Valclusa's womb,
  Baptised at birth upon her native stream.

Sorga is never still;
The banks partake its thrill.
Enchanted clumps of laurel arch its sky,
  And cool the rushing glades,
As souls from Nature fly
  To these protecting shades.
'Twas here a moon-lit wave
Daphne, the laurel nymph, her being gave.
  With sighs that waft contagious fire,
Hermes beheld her in the light of love
That filled the grove;
  And taught her earth's affections on his lyre.

Daphne her simple name,
Not she of classic fame

Whom the young god, beholding with desire,
  Pursued from east to west,
And with too hot a fire
  The virgin charms carest,
Dissolving her in flame,
A laurel only to preserve her name;
  Not she, but one as undefil'd;
In virgin thought and chastity of heart
  Her counterpart;
Of river-god and earth, like her, the child.

CHORUS.

The fiery god whose days
Were scantier than his rays,
No more with arts, though in full lustre orbed,
  Unwary nymph allures,
Nor, in himself absorbed,
  Her simple love conjures;
Let only to display
His grace and beauty to the light of day.
  For Fate was crowded in the cast,
Consigning gods to sepulchres divine,
To ever shine
  As monuments of power that ruled the past.

As once, in heaven-fought wars,
No longer clash the stars,
But sweep the endless orbits, each apart,
   Still fiefs of hidden Fate,
Whom nothing lives to thwart,
   Whom none can penetrate.
Imaged in bold relief
As more than Nature's independent chief,
   Is now the influx of a wave,
Where floats a new and solitary throne,
For One alone,
   His turn wide Nature's suffrages to brave.

II.

VALCLUSA.

WHY in that breast of tepid clay, whose shape
The soul assumes to soon or late escape,
Didst thou, O Hermes, thy affections train :
For constant joy can never there remain !
In Daphne's image why thy soul attire,
To waste away in impotent desire,
To wait, as others wait whom death assails,
For unreturning hope whose errand fails?
Thou diest, so canst not parley with the fair
Who touch not what they tread on, earth or air :
They see thy face, O Hermes, they admire
Thy human vastness, thy enrapturing fire,
They see thy form with eyes they cannot wean ;
They hear thy voice, thy voice's cadence glean,
Though not with ears that deafen in the blast,
Though not with hearts that vanish in the past.

O Hermes, rather faint than so infect
Thy soul with love's immortal dialect!
We die not who hold converse in its strain,
Though like to thee beset with other's pain:
But thou wilt in the midst of it expire
And leave behind its uttermost desire.
Shouldst thou the love of nymph immortal win,
Thy loss exceeds the penalty of sin:
That, time condones, erasing with a blot;
But love eternal man recovers not,
Unless perchance he bear a thousand pains
Before a foretaste of delight he gains,
While we exist for only life's excess,
Born happy to live on in happiness.

Now are the hours alone;
They mourn for Daphne gone.
Nature the silent obsequy attends
   When spirits pure depart,
And some slight token sends
   Consoling to the heart.
But Daphne's days begun,
She took fond leave of earth at set of sun,
   And went on the returning beams,
With holy art to decorate above
The dome of love,
   And paint its sober disc with coloured dreams.

Hermes loved her alone;
Daphne the only one.
Ideal rapture, that consumes in fire
   All utterances of thought,
All breathings of desire,
   The only dower she brought.
Nature is sad around:
A mourning voice that utters not a sound!
   Where was the tenant of his mind?
In every laurel with a love divine
He saw her shrine:
An empty heaven by Daphne left behind.

CHORUS.

But now was Daphne's part
To tend the broken heart!
As in her hand a vase some vestal bears,—
   On its translucid glow
Her finger's shade appears,
   As there to stanch the flow;
For love itself she saw
Ooze at the irremediable flaw.
   And still against her breast she kept
The broken heart, its bursting love to stay,
Its smart allay,
   As at the well of sympathy it wept.

Her sisters, fair and bright,
Within the arch of light
Depict earth's sorrow on the canopy,
   And graceful hours beguile,
That angels, passing by,
   May sadden as they smile.
Her sisters, born of day
To gild humanity and pass away,
   Are there the well-known sigh to tend,—
The earnest part of mortal man's alloy,
Though not his joy,—
   And in the distant choir its sweetness spend.

Begot as fancy broods
In Nature's dreamy moods,
On them the world imprints its early trace.
   They wear a look of love
In sadness on their face,
   To plead man's griefs above.
Like Daphne, good and fair,
Children of joy though natives of despair,
   Art dwells in their seraphic eyes,
Transposing all they gaze upon with pain,
To that vast plain
   Which holds the drifted glory of the skies.

VALCLUSA.

These days in heaven begin
Without a wish to sin.
Thence Daphne, by no wayward fancy led,
   Her wondering look bestows
On tears by woman shed,
   And so all pity knows.
O symbols of distress!
Why hide your meaning from the angel's guess?
   But no repining heart replies,
While anguish that no likeness has above,
Is borne for love
   That brighter burns the surer that it dies.

Her eyes meander long
Her olden haunts among.
At length they spy a woman on the road,
   With looks beset with fear:
No place to rest the load
   That broken hearts must bear.
Not one for pity's sake
Her single sorrow willing to partake.
   Madeline the name the wanderer bore,
Told to the sky above, to earth below,
For all to know
   Her maiden name accorded her no more.

CHORUS.

Shall, then, no hand of love,
Save only that above,
Alight with healing touch the wound to hide?
   No gentle breath be nigh,
Like comfort at her side,
   With sigh to mingle sigh
O'er the soul-setting blush?
That shadow virtue casts herself to crush!
   O for a voice, a single tone
To move the lover in his steadfast pride
Toward that sweet bride,
   And soothe the power to vengeance slowly prone!

VALCLUSA.

Not wedded to his lore
Should man his help implore,
Was Hermes, summoned now his prince to brave,
   To brook his cold disdain,
The innocent to save
   From virtue's mystic stain.
Unknown to earthly power,
His utmost gift as yet the poet's dower,
   The prince in terror held his race,
And barred at his approach the castle-gate,
Until too late
   To snatch the victim of defiled embrace.

Those turrets old as war
Outvie the heights afar.
A potentate wields all their dreaded power,
   Inherits all their frown;
Lord of a conqueror's tower:
   Upon his brow a crown.
Armour, deserted shell,
Behind whose vizor ghostly heroes dwell,
   Haunts every nook in mute array;
Skulls drive their antlers through the upper space,
And hail the chase:
   Ensigns of peace and war on holiday.

How long outlast man's life
These weapons of his strife!
On iron arm the battered shield is slung
   That broke the axe's fall;
On iron hands are hung
   Spears pointing to the wall.
The helmet's shivered crest
Records the blow that gave a spirit rest.
   Here link to link of woven chain,
There scale to scale, is mailèd coat, akin
To serpent's skin.
   Cast by the young in haste of battle slain.

In carved and gilded case,
Rare relics of a race,
Bestowed with care, their fabled story tell.
   The empty tankard stands,
As if beneath a spell,
   In fast tradition's hands.
The gentle crucifix
With it and baser emblems deigns to mix.
   In panels hung, to likeness true,
Are saints and soldiers, counting back their crimes
To farthest times,
   With dauntless eyes that outrage still pursue.

Oft there did Hermes' feet
A lively welcome greet:
Nor now the prince could long deny a name
   Whose praise the nations spoke,
Whose words like waves of flame
   On every listener broke.
But lawless love had lit
The prince's breast, and yet must ravage it.
   Could words avert its blind intent,
Could they instate, where fed a lustful fire,
The just desire,
   Or set a bound to his impetuous bent?

Still at no distant day,—
More earnest by delay,—
The poet greets the despot face to face,
　With look that look refutes:
With less than wonted grace
　His eye the crime imputes.
And then comes sense of right
To wrestle, singly, with a ruler's might.
　What though with honest prayer he try
To touch the icy heart, as with the rays
Of summer days;
　A frozen shield can radiant souls defy.

O Waste of Words! how guile
Can cross thee with a smile;
Thy storms repress, thy thunder-signs deride,
　Thy lightning-stroke repel,
And turn its flash aside,
　Though vengeance it foretel!
But had some prophet raved
His oracles had not the victim saved.
　So high the sphere of his estate,
The prince heard, unabashed, the words that blame,
To hring no shame,
　And Hermes he dismissed with courteous hate.

What hand outstretched shall move
The heart to beat in love ?
This Hermes asks of tower-embattled skies,
 Beyond where banners float.
Below he bends his eyes.
 A vision fills the moat :
No hand outstretched to save ;
Skies, tower-embattled, trembling with the wave.
 The absent hand he understood ;
The sign was given, of it the portent found,
That he should sound
 The bearings of a yet unfathomed flood !

III.

VALCLUSA.

When sages speak how graceful is debate;
Their words the ministers, themselves the state.
As heaven disposes so the work is done,
The trust consigned to human hands alone.
But where the prince, propped up with equal might
For good or harm, who bends himself to right?
Yet on the meanest scenes that pass below
May Heaven her utmost vigilance bestow,
With constant aid the weaker may surprise,
The more when man the wrong cannot chastise.
Then Nature's rule may make a solemn pause,
And Heaven insert her peremptory clause.
So is it now; the titled Sire who reigns,
For one brief hour a puny struggle feigns.
Not in a word his wonders he creates;
Not in a word his works he desolates.

Yet if once slow to choose a fitting site
For worlds that number now the infinite,
There may be days when seeming to vacate
A home so far, so kingly an estate,
He journeys thence to cast a tyrant down,
And turn to dust his sceptre and his crown.
In storms of fire, as lightning's aspect stern
That many orbs his orders may discern,
In storms of light, the lightnings split in twain
That man may seek his purposes in vain,
Kind in his ire, the harmless dove he spares;
His bounty with the lone and helpless shares.
When rains descend, when to and fro are driven
Tempests of spray from kindred waters riven,
When sulky night herself the earth invest,
He turns the half-fledged sparrow in its nest.
So now a harvest droops, now lowers a sky,
And air sails under stress of sorcery.
Meteors let loose, from their allegiance rush;
The paler planets like the redder flush;
The shut-up lava-spouts resume their scope,
And mortal dread is in the place of hope.
Yet farther off, beyond the golden belt
Of habitable heaven, a doom is felt.
Nymphs, angels now, who earth remember well,
Are moved to tears by the prevailing spell.

As when the wind from o'er the mountain flows
Man weeps and yet no cause for sorrow knows,
Tears from their sobered hearts, spontaneous flung,
Course down their cheeks as fast as pearls unstrung.
So dense the blight the very angels mope:
And Daphne knows the sudden loss of hope.
Unused before to feel the drag of doom,
She paces heaven as in a convent-room,
Till her sad thoughts towards Madeline oscillate,
And point at her, the loadstone of her fate.

By Eden's drooping site,
Fit scene of many a rite,
Freighted with doom by Nature's titled Sire,
   A star was on its road
Bristling with quills of fire
   'Neath its unwonted load,—
As if the orb of day
Drove night before it on the solar way.
   The magi, from their holy hill
Looked up towards Oromasdes' paveless seat,—
Unreached retreat!
   Prompt to observe and minister his will.

Then, mystic figures ran
Across the talisman,

While travelled past that meteor of fire,
   The symbol pure and blessed
Of Nature's titled Sire,
   To the elect addressed.
They followed it with eyes
Fixed on its glory as it clove the skies:
   At length the marvel, boding good,
Rested above, enconing half its glow
On all below,
   While over Hermes' lowly home it stood.

" Since thy bright horoscope
Reflects wing-gifted hope
Where glory wanders; where its toils expire
   For ever-growing joy,
And infinite desire
   That earth cannot alloy;
We bear thee great reward:
' From Oromasdes to the new-born bard!'
   We (so they spake) thy genius greet!
We, the proud magi of an ancient creed,
To meet thy need,
   Lay now our priceless offerings at thy feet.

" The East, that fades not, wears
An aspect of old years.

The empty crater, the ash-littered mount,
  But more, the legend rife
That here was Nature's fount,
  Her crucible of life,
Ere yet extinct the spells
Wherein the magic of creation dwells,
  To man in sad rehearsal plead;
The more that now his days are hoary grown,
And youth is flown:
  Gone first, the avant-courier to the dead.

" Skies soft as amethyst,
Where floats the golden mist,
(As when the order of man's days began),
  Shower down the planet's rays
To gild the talisman
  While the magician prays,
And with their influent gleams
Transfix the coruscating disc with beams.
  Through this the magian works the charm
To speed a noble sorrow, or consign
To stars malign
  The cruel heart that asks another's harm.

" Skilled in all magic gear,
The blazoned seal we bear.

By its occult divinings, not for ill,
   The inmates of the grave
Are subject to our will;
   Beneath the naked wave
The passionless who sleep,
As past their bier the breaking waters creep,
   Give up their startled souls in fright
At its enchantments; hurried from their rest
At our behest,
   And in pale terror visioned on the night.

" On this true talisman,
Fate's pre-concerted plan
And the celestial circle harmonise.
   On it the clusters burn
That nightly set and rise,
   And in their orbits turn.
So let its magic spell
Henceforth in thee as in the planets dwell!"
   Thus spake the magi and the prize
Gave up that from a distant land they bore,
Fraught with a lore
   Of times to come transcending man's surmise.

IV.

CHORUS.

CAN such a tale of love
Fail human hearts to move?
Have not the old a tear for Madeline;
  For the frail infant riven
  From virtue's ancient shrine
    And into exile driven?
A wanderer with her shame,
In far-off lands she hides her maiden name!
  The young may stray; O break their fall,
Not the weak soul its nursery expel
If it rebel,
  But take it back ere lost beyond recal!

VALCLUSA.

The watchful angels crave
That lovely soul to save.

Said Daphne: "Hermes once my love desired:
  Nor would my wish deny,—
By nobler love inspired,—
  To fetch her to the sky."
This thought her peace devours;
It wings with sympathy the new-born hours.
  Nor vain the web of grace it wove:
She held the thread that turned at ebb of tide
A fate aside,
  To drag the drowning from the wreck of love.

CHORUS.

Let drop no word of scorn
On Madeline the forlorn,
But mourn her; yet her name may be divine;
  Her sin may be condoned:
There is a Madeline
  Among the saints enthroned.
This earthly flower, so fair,
Exhaled a perfume as it rode the air;
  In modesty was hung its head.
But one who saw the early bud expand
Put out his hand
  And plucked the nestled germ ere it had spread.

VALCLUSA.

Then Daphne's sweet desire
Was flashed on Hermes' lyre,
Whose throb replied : To Madeline's succour hie !
   She of celestial race
Who wished for once to die,
   As saints have done in grace,
Leaves heaven without a sigh
To bear young Madeline back with her on high.
   Rejoicing in her course she chose
The poet's soul for her nativity,
To live and die
   Environed by his glory to the close.

She long had pined in vain
To share in woman's pain,
With longings that in virtue only burn ;
   To taste for once of death,
And share the poet's urn ;
   And share the withered wreath.
Now, her loved task to keep
A soul pursued in waking and in sleep,
   She blushed into the poet's sight,
Born at the moment to the good decreed ;
The hour of need ;
   Cleaving with luminosity the night.

V.

VALCLUSA.

Now with a sense that opens on the space
Of scenes too far for vision to retrace,
Shall Hermes with his spells half Nature bind,
At least where laws run counter to his mind.
He bids the wheel of fate make half a round:
How many hearts fall palsied on the ground!
But one which in its socket quivers still,
Adverse to justice and its grinding will,
Hermes reserves for yet one more appeal,
Ere the last writ of fate receive its seal.
Then shall the wheel, which at his order turns,
Crush the hard heart that human nature spurns.

It was the hour of night
When stars defer their light,

And moons to some far hiding-place retire,
　But in the poet's mind
Leave all their dreamy fire.
　There, paths the comets find;
There, suns that rule the day
Extend the utmost uses of their ray.
　There angels, wont his soul to range,
Pass in and out; perhaps to where they stray
The nearer way;
　And in abstraction lost scarce note the change.

Nor know they how to hide
The thoughts on which they glide,
Their inmost visions opened to his eyes
　With all the love they dream:
Heaven's fondest reveries
　Allowed on him to gleam.
The story in their face,
The poet's simple task its plot to trace,
　It tells itself from first to last,
And in their heart he reads the episode,
Its blest abode,
　That bids them on their errand wander past.

Though night all else devour
It is the poet's hour.

All sinking Nature singly to sustain,
   He things anew creates;
But haunted still by pain
   That never dissipates,
And summoned still by sin,
While rapt discourse and minstrelsy begin.
   As the world's splendour sinks away,
And drowsy mortals in the drug of sleep
Their senses steep,
   He gathers up the fragments of a day.

Nor in those solitudes
Madeline his sight eludes.
She pensive leans against the baffling blast,
   While only he is left
To watch, to pray, to fast,
   To mourn for the bereft.
Sustained by love, he pours
The wisdom of his soul along the hours
   To save her from a worse estate;
While her the warning mocks to sin no more,
And long deplore
   The one false step that made her desolate.

In that bewildering storm
He viewed her half-nude form.

She poured out no lament, but sorely wept,
  As woman only weeps
O'er others' vows unkept,
  While hers she fondly keeps,
And at her heart retains,
The more another's pride her love disdains.
  To save her, not as man provides,
For heaven to every human aim appends
Her private ends,
  The envied task to Daphne he confides.

So comes this sylph of song
Where earth's fair daughters throng
Their virgin hours in chastity to spend;
  The passions, as they glow,
With holiness to blend,
  And turn from life below.
They breathe their first desire
Like angels with an evangelic fire,
  But soon or late, with loving arms,
Accept a partner in the dance of sin,
To death begin,
  And drift away from heaven's dissolving charms.

In tinted marble shaped,
In tinted vesture draped,

Leans Daphne's statue o'er her natal stream,
   When, like the northern light
Filtering through evening's dream,
   Her face grows rosy bright.
The wings irradiate,
And ever as they glow new soul create.
   "Behold," said she, "I come again
By thy consent, to beckon artless vice
To paradise,
   And link by link whirl back its broken chain."

The poet scarce replies,
Yet thinks how soon the ties
Are loosed that bind an angel to her home,
   Though with a silent pride,
That echoes worlds to come,
   He sees her sorrow's bride.
"Ah! sad," said he, "the day:
Madeline, like thee, from home is far away,
   But, brooding over woes untold,
She sits in mourning like a haughty saint
Without complaint,
   Roofless as pilgrims in the time of old."

Meantime his heart that strove
With a seditious love,

Did he deny its rapture to betray.
   To more than mortal gain
The angel points the way:
   Nor his vexed heart in vain
To charity had grown,
And to another's woes subscribed its own.
   Enlisted in the sacred cause,
His love is on the altar, where, like gusts,
All mortal lusts,
   By holiness surprised, for ever pause.

VI.

VALCLUSA.

Genius of heart, that fags and never tires,
The source of all beneficent desires,
That not for love's award in beauty lives,
Or those delights which wealth or glory gives;
Not lured to sip an angel's tepid kiss
Lest the mild rapture reach forbidden bliss:
Why thus from selfish joys thy spirit turn,
While yet for others' good its cravings burn?
Man for himself an ample treasure hides
Ere for his meanest neighbour he provides.
In charity both rise and set thy days,
And so thy ways transcend all others' ways.
Nature thy sister rather than thy spouse,
In purity sustains thy noble house.

Madeline.

Be there abodes above the untouched sky,
Of these soft filtering vales the canopy,
Beyond the lofty shrine whereby our eyes
Are drawn up in half-conscious reveries
Whereof we find no purpose, yet adore,
Nor care, when freed, their meaning to explore;
Be there abodes for which must ever pine
A sacred heart endowed with love like thine,
May'st thou ascend, embalmed in sweets and spice,
And better life attain in paradise!

Now that her sandalled feet
The earth's chill surface meet,
Is Daphne conscious of her heart's rebound.
  It pulsates in the fear,
That hems a virgin round,
  Of dangers ever near,
Some that the darkness hides,
Some that the conscience to the soul confides.
  And she must shudder with the dread
Of ghostly passions, visitants of sleep,
In forms that weep;
  And do harsh penance in another's stead.

On angel-errantry
Proudly she takes the sky.

Soaring she kens with large-eyed glance a seat
   Where steps like wave on wave
A portal seemed to beat;
   Where few admittance crave.
There sat a girlish form
Wrecked on a convent by the driving storm.
   Her fingers shaped in beauty's dream
Languished in grief, of all their play bereft,
As in their cleft
   They held a cheek, the bed of sorrow's stream.

Her arms like columns fair
Were shrouded by her hair.
As the torn ivy hangs disconsolate,
   The locks were tossed and blown,
And beat against the gate
   A music of their own.
Youths hurrying by the spires
That upward point the frigid nun's desires
   From cloistered hearths to skies that burn,
Pause at her charms as things put in their way
For pleasant play,
   Easy to take as easy to return.

Before that convent gate
No suppliant she sate;

Her sins as yet for penitence too few.
  Her lover's cherished wiles
On her their spell renew,
  And stop but when she smiles.
An interval of pain,
And they rehearse their witchery again.
  Deep lies the well of misery,
But deeper still its spring that yet must flow
Through rocks below,
  Till sorrow's source has run its waters dry.

With gentle words that strove
To feign the voice of love,
Intoned in other tongues to pity's sound,
  Youths stopped their suit to press,
To open wide her wound,
  To prey on her distress.
Not long their wit they task
To find she little dreams of what they ask!
  No providence their steps decreed
To solace or seduce the broken heart,
And they depart;
  Leaving to droop and die the bended reed.

Vice in a tongue unknown
Now claims her for its own.

But on a rack her soul already lies
   Its torture to endure,
Nor shall love's votaries
   Its tainted use procure.
They feel for her distress
Yet sigh to damn her more, themselves to bless.
   But to enticing gestures blind,
Her eyes are fondly sunk in memory's pit,
To fathom it,
   And in its cheerless gulf her lover find.

And as she sits unmoved,
So loving, so unloved,
And lone as only love can lonely be,
   The youths walk to and fro,
And turn her face to see,
   And ask for yes or no.
Too mild in words to chide,
With piteous glance her eyes she opens wide.
   See they in hers a sister's end?
The dread strikes home and they return no more,
Smit to the core,
   Lest equal shame on their own house descend.

CHORUS.

And must she now, still pure,
The shocks of vice endure?

O that her ears could to her soul disclose
  The one once loving sound!
But farewell now repose
  Except in holy ground!
Let her the vigil keep
Till at the grave her heart sinks into sleep,
  And her last tears put out its flame.
Then shall the reddened eyes be turned to stone;
And grief alone
  In marble live to weep her mortal shame.

VALCLUSA.

Must the deserted one
Be ever thus alone?
Not if her soul emerge again from night
  To face its former pride,
To question it aright
  And its resolves abide!
Akin to her distress
The weeping sky pours on her its caress;
  And she, so beautiful in form,
Drips like a naiad watered by a cloud;
Her spirit proud
  Baited by gusts set at her by the storm.

But why should she complain?
The lilies bear the rain,
And courteous earth absolves the heaven of wrong.
   Will no kind sky restrain
The lowering thoughts that throng
   To flood her breast with pain?
Above the mountain crests,
Above the storm, the watchful angel rests.
   The mists aside their curtain throw;
Her glance descends and like the lightning's ball
Pursues its fall,
   And Madeline's face illumines in its glow.

VII.

VALCLUSA.

Be memory the soul that dieth not
Lest love, the only joy, should be forgot,
Be memory the life beyond the grave
That beareth hence the little it would save,
Then Madeline surely saw all anguish close;
Saw love as one who from the dead arose.

Pure is the Alpine snow;
Not night can hide its glow:
Self-luminous along the rayless waste!
   Yet eyes than frosted light
More lustrous and more chaste,
   On Madeline pour their sight.
Round her the angel flings
Two loving arms, while droop two silvery wings.

Still Madeline all that love repels,
Though it was missed beyond the firmament,
Whence it was sent
   To save for heaven the favourite who rebels.

Madeline, still sick and chill,
Was prone to brood on ill;
But not for this an angel's love she spurned:
   A shame, with eyes abashed,
Her cheeks to hectic turned,
   And through their pallor flashed.
Then spoke with artless skill
That draws a weaker to a firmer will,
   The looks that mourn a soul's distress.
Nor words, though more than syren-like their strain,
Can tell again
   The epithets that holy eyes express!

And these could Madeline bear,
Still unreleased the tear?
Yet why renew the sympathetic tie
   If hope in her be dead?
Her soul's sad malady
   To one so taintless spread?
More easy to impart
The sure infection than allay its smart!

Madeline.

So thought she volubly, so spoke
Within her soul, that tablet which records
The silent words.
   At length the noiseless dialogue she broke.

" Not like to mine thy race !
Thy steps imprint no trace.
Mine sink into the mire ; an outcast's feet
   Their naked stamp betray
The curious eye to greet,
   Though lonesome be their way.
Yet was I never poor
Till he who loved me forced my father's door.
   Thou knowest the tale of my disgrace :
The ruby ring that this wan finger wore
His image bore.
   Now pale its glow and dim its living face.

" O messenger of love
Thy gentle arms remove !
Not all thy purity can re-engraft
   The flower that buds no more ;
Not all thy heavenly craft
   Its virtue can restore.
Ah blest were it to lie
Upon thy neck, these eyelids close, and die !

Few tears these spendthrift eyes can spare.
Alone the ways of confidence are sweet
When equals meet:
But joy and sorrow little have to share.

" Leave me that I may rove
Unwatched by others' love,
And drag my load of life from all away,
To every eye unknown.
Leave me alone to stray,
Till death shall take his own.
No blush can then retrace
The crimson cloud that drifts before my face,
Nor more the pallid cheek assail.
In kindness leave me to resign my breath
Alone to death;
In solitude of soul his coming hail!

" From home I turn my face
Where tears my name displace.
Here is the vagrant welcome to a tomb,
With her memorial shame
Inscribed within her womb:
Beyond the reach of blame.
O leave me on this spot;
Or where I yet may wander, follow not!

For thou art decked in newest light;
A pity in thine eye that ever dwells
Thy nature tells:
Not death's cold angel on her downward flight!

" Leave me, yet with thee take,
For both my parents' sake,
This broken heart, to them its love return.
　Be thou its sanctuary,
Be thou its vital urn;
　But leave me here to die.
No child to them is left:
Of honour robbed of all are they bereft.
　And if their prayer by thee be blest,
And they their child have asked thee to restore,
Return no more
　Till thou canst say her spirit is at rest.

" O guardian of my home,
Say not that thou hast come
To lead me hence: my father's voice I hear
　And dread its stifled tone!
My mother's love I fear
　When left with her alone!
On death my prayer remains,
That they may weep once more then end their pains.

And couldst thou to the loved again
His peace of mind restore, when I am dust,
In heaven his trust ;
   Then should immortal hope my end sustain."

As dreams o'er conscience sweep
Ere closed the gates of sleep ;
As winds the flooded meadow brush along
   Where water-blossoms bloom,
She poured her raptured song,
   And wailed her maiden doom.
Within the angel's ear
Sank deep the words, to her than heaven more dear.
   Madeline had told her tale again,
But now the choking, intermittent sob
With piteous throb,
   Drowns in its swell the current of her pain.

As thus her heart repines
On Daphne she reclines.
Now with a gasp she yields her panting breath,
   Now in rehearsal slow
Repeats the sigh of death :
   Life's ending ebb and flow.
O'er her the angel bends
To learn how ever-sobbing languor ends :

She fears the life may suffer wreck,
And glide, unconscious, past its level brink,
To sink and sink,
Until the universe seem but a speck.

Madeline has ceased to stray
Along the conscious way,
She sinking lightly on oblivion's car,
  With loosened reins her palm
Entangled, as afar
  She skims the ethereal calm.
Her yet tremendous fate
No obstacles betray, no dreams relate :
  But hushed in that mysterious sleep,
Her passions in unbroken billows rest,
Nor foams their crest :
  Forbade to stir on the enchanted deep.

Now safe across the bar,
No shoals her course to mar,
The soul has rest, that daily else must die.
  And as its living flame
Within the tomb may lie
  To answer to its name,
Her body she enshrouds
Beside the tempest in the passing clouds,—

Those cerements of a troubled night!
So takes she part with universal rest,
And like the blest
　　Her inner temple guards with lamp and light.

Becalmed the moments creep;
Her tears drop off, asleep.
Her couching eyelids fringe the placid cheek.
　　A holy fervour feeds
Her bosom orbed and meek:
　　The peace her spirit needs.
The giver of all alms
With thrill of strange delight her heart embalms.
　　Like music on the wane, she drops
Into a wondrous pause, and, full of life
Without its strife,
　　Absorbs the bliss of heaven while being stops.

VIII.

VALCLUSA.

Now clinging ice-like are those marble arms
To Daphne's neck, while Daphne's bosom warms
Both hearts, and both to sympathy confides:
With twofold grace from death the dying hides.
The bard exults in that benign embrace:
Madeline with peace eternal face to face.
He turns his eyes, obstructed by a tear,
On scenes she shared, a stranger then to fear,
Now such as in a dream the glance retakes
When at a passing thought the past awakes:
Returned from sleep again the pleasance seen,
Yet still the past, the something which has been.
But as in body she is far removed
From him who robbed her, far from scenes she loved,
So her seducer gives to her no thought,
But masked in revels sets her woes at nought.

Through her inured yet more to virgin pain,
He plots the like immaculate to stain;
His riper vows on innocence to thrust:
The purer found, the sweeter to his lust.
So fresh affections dreams he to decoy,
And swell the numbers ever lost to joy!
But now a warning hand is raised to strike,
And Heaven, who governs justly all alike,
Scatters a misty blight that gathers round,
Than lust more deadly, denser than the ground;
A blight that in the east like fog begins,
But is a remnant of man's early sins.
No moon stands half-way towards the seat of war
Unseen the lazulite and inlaid star,
Along the sable-blue no spark betrays
The candid halo of so many rays.
Heaven has retired, mankind to stupefy
Like heaps of wretches buried ere they die.
As if despair had grown within the land
Erect in night the bristled forests stand;
The leafless boughs like arms dart into space,
To feel their way while death comes on apace;
The waters hide their flow, their murmurs hush,
For silence hearkening, conscious of its gush.
A one last light remembered, from that spot
Irradiates the universal blot.

Madeline. 61

That none may look upon their future home:
The sky dismantled like a cindered dome.
One heavenless depth where souls may laugh or pray:
From God to man a silence all the way.

Illustrious for crime
Through centuries of time,
Its sanctuary the moated castle rears;
  But there no memory weeps:
The drudgery of tears
  Scorned by the lord who sleeps.
Dreams he a poet's powers
Can rule him in his solitary towers?
  Now summoned to atone for sin
Harsh incantations reach him from afar
With threats of war,
  Whose harbingers the sullen strife begin.

To those who truly grieve
The world yields some reprieve:
It shares a slumber where all censures end.
  To those who ought to weep
Can that same world extend
  The liberty of sleep?
Her once fond lord might tell!
As Madeline sank to rest a meteor fell

From tower-embattled skies, and shone
Upon the waters that his home intrenched;
Within them quenched:
   Circling the billows in their spreading zone.

Within those towers remote
The drowsy lord it smote;
The shores of sleep uprooting from repose.
   As Madeline sank to bliss,
On him the waves arose.
   In their retreating hiss
He hears the knell of fate,
And its far echo, woman's dreaded hate.
   He listens to the distant chime:
When its last tremor strikes the silent sense
To impotence,
   He travels still the desert path of time.

The warning strikes more deep
Poured on him in his sleep.
And as he hears the waves in their rebound,
   And feels their surging boom,
He sees the spray surround
   The messengers of doom,
Who stand in ranks to wage
On him the menace, wrapped in choral rage.

And as his soul these scenes embroil,
The serpents tangled in the Furies' hair
Desert their lair,
Fall to the couch and round his forehead coil.

A deadly sweat bestrews
His face with icy dews.
Thick as the tears that wet a cavern wall,
And race the dripping rain,
From off his brow they fall;
Swell up and drop again.
Like tendrils of a vine
He feels the reptiles round his conscience twine
And revel in a future state,
The Furies mustered in the circling row,
With looks that glow,
And hearts that riot in the pangs of hate.

Their eyes, that inly brood,
Run down with molten blood,
Whose splash corrodes the armour of his sleep :
Bent over him like age,
Not knowing that they weep,
They empty out their rage.
They curse him by the skies,
They curse him by the towers whereinhe lies.

He trembles at the words of fate,
And draws the hot infection of their breath,
Whose touch brings death
   His pride to blight, his house to desolate.

They scatter in his path
The emblems of their wrath.
Aghast, his soul beholds their lurid brands
   Point out the exile's way
To lone, untravelled lands
   That never look on day.
Nor youth, nor beauty's charm,
Their just intent can soften or disarm.
   What they dispose must needs befal;
More drear than the funereal pomp of man
The work they plan :
   Lightning their torch and night their sable pall.

They lay the fatal hand,
They set its tightened band
Upon his heart; they barter nod for nod,
   And fix, with fingers tall,
The fiat of a god
   Against his chamber wall.
The shadow of his doom
He gazes on till twilight spans the room.

Across his heart a hand remains,
Whence hourly grows the superstitious fear
That death is near;
A dread that to the end his soul retains.

IX.

VALCLUSA.

Now from the orgies held at dead of night,
By him contrived, the bard averts his sight,
Loth long to watch how that malignant crew
Performed a task best never to renew.
The warning over, which unaided sleep
 Had not evoked, though left to phrensy's keep,
There let it work and of the soul regain
A seed of righteous love, a sand-sized grain;
There let it burst and strike, there bud and blow,
And what its holy worth in blossom show.
Meantime,—to where two flowers exude their light,
Fluttering like burrs upon the edge of flight,
Let us return, and with the Furies' hiss
Contrast the silent scenery of bliss.

Madeline.

On Madeline's peaceful eyes
Drops fresh as from the skies
A tropical affection with its rays.
  The angel's watchful face
Leans over her and prays;
  And like the moon in space
With inspiration burns,
Reflecting light whichever way it turns.
  The hour that Daphne waits is come:
Two swan-like wings with equal grace expand
At her command,
  To bear the sleeper to the poet's home.

Where lie the hopeful lands
On which his palace stands?
Whither now tends the flight of this fond pair?
  Beyond the mountain chains,
Those cities of the air;
  Beyond the cereal plains.
They reach the sky-blue clime
That bubbles round a theatre of crime,
  The scenes expanding as they rise;
Above one star, under another stray;
And on their way,
  Not stopping, brush the verge of paradise.

Not from the azure dome
Is seen his lowly home;
Yet where the poet finds an earthly rest
    Cones of prophetic light
Obey his mild behest,
    As escorts of his sight;
Couriers that lead afar
Into the colours of the double star.
    Else wasted in the ephemeral way,
The wonders as they cease, like gusts that blew,
In him renew
    The transient glories of their mild decay.

That hour a message brings
Fresh from the angel's wings
Whose downy stroke has checked the tempest's stride.
    The problem it resolves,
Why, moving side by side,
    A double soul revolves
Within the upper night.
There all is dark, save where salutes his sight
    That shape, meandering as a cloud,
Whirled like the driven snow athwart some heath,
Where wintry death
    In wild perennial flowerets decks the shroud.

His soul the vision greets;
In prayer the hour he meets.
But whence his faith in holy courts to pray?
　Can he the lost defend,
The sentence passed, delay;
　The broken spirit mend?
Alas, in sober thought,
What mortal yet a miracle has wrought?
　Beyond a poet's utmost skill!
Now slow revenge must Madeline's will controul,
And bend her soul
　Some deed of utmost horror to fulfil.

But this was a decree
No prescience could foresee.
The world of fate in distant darkness dwells,
　Its ways to vision sealed:
Nor mortal ever spells
　What there lies unrevealed.
But Madeline past it sweeps,
She drowns within its ether while she sleeps,
　Unheard the breaking of its waves.
Meantime, in mercy for affections riven,
Is pardon given
　At heaven's high font to her whose soul it laves.

And now knows Madeline
A change to life divine.
The ever-sure elixir that distils
   Through her, in rising dew,
Condones all mortal ills;
   Those who partake it few.
Fate holds an empire here;
To all occult the marches of her sphere.
   The foe of life her virtue stuns,
Incanting, in the passing of a breath,
The sting of death,
   Which shrivels up before its poison runs.

Immortal ecstasy
Fills the all-bracing sky;
It clings to those who once its ether taste,
   That they to endless time
May perish not, nor waste
   In energy sublime.
But she who now has clomb
The purple arch that overlaps the tomb,
   Is made amenable to fate,
To be her own avenger; not unscathed!
Her fingers bathed
   In human gore, the implements of hate.

X.

VALCLUSA.

LIKE stars that settle in the firmament,
On Sorga's bank there glitters many a tent.
In one lies Madeline yet in slumber stilled;
Those round about by guardian angels filled.
Such was the poet's thought, though heaven's the plan:
The holy scene invisible to man.
For Madeline now has not a mortal's place
But shares while yet on earth an equal grace
With those whose tents her hospital surround,
Left here till fully healed her smarting wound!
The indignant sense retained as just and fit
To do the deed that best avenges it;
The human impulse held, and left to time;
Her soul no more responsible for crime.
Even now on her oblivious eyes are shed,
In mock appearance, joys for ever fled,
That when her life may back to sense return
The maddening wrong in her may deeper burn.

Sleep in his sluggish folds
The favoured captive holds,
Till earth for the adopted of the sky
    Fit resting-place provides ;
She, there unsensed, to lie
    As some pale cloud that strides,
Belated on its way,
The purple vault at early break of day.
    She dreads no sun whose arrows stream
Along the east to pierce her eyes with light,
And give to flight
    The now fair phantoms of her childish dream.

Seven streams of light had run
In glory from the sun,
As open curtains over her who sleeps,
    Drawn by the sorcerer's hand
Who at her slumber peeps
    To touch her with his wand,
And at its magic stroke
The morning dream ere waking to invoke.
    The early days which yet she knew,
Like pictures in the spirit's looking-glass,
Her gaze repass,
    And elder tidings of her love renew.

Scenes fresh as yester-morn
Her pleasant state adorn,
As if the lovely hours, not wholly gone,
  But only overcast,
In fresh enchantment shone,
  As evermore to last.
Joys tiring of their urn,
Too perfect in their parts, to life return.
  With them the play its curtain lifts,
An instant scarce permitted to engage
The airy stage,
  Lest in it melt the phantoms ere it shifts.

Yet it was like a play
On some long holiday.
The scenes once blest and once the raptures known,
  Return to her untold,
As if they were her own,
  And purest days unfold.
Not strange the poor pretence
They offer back to her of innocence.
  The false to clasp, the true evade,
Through Nature's mask she looks on paradise
Without surprise;
  Trailing her soul alongside as her shade.

CHORUS.

What company is sleep
For lonely hearts to keep !
The dream is day when truth walks out of sight ;
   When it comes back again,
The dream sinks into night,
   Its pleasure into pain.
Young memory runs away
As in the sunny meads the children play.
   Is rapture, then, let out on hire,
To sink into its sorrow like a tide
In all its pride,
   And in its flush of ecstasy expire?

A chorus softly sang,
The sober warning rang,
But only joy could listen to the strain,
   And not the meaning catch.
The warning rang again
   But not the sense to match.
The penalty of sleep,
To smile in sorrow and in joy to weep !
   O magical deceiver, stay ;
Illusion all, though true thy mocking mime,
Except to time :
   Of all that happens thou canst change the day !

Madeline.

Why should the sleeper mourn?
All leads to sorrow's bourn!
She sees a youth like her of tender years.
   Is it his air of grace,
The charm her lover wears?
   She gazes on his face;
The lineaments the same;
But when she hears his voice she knows his name.
   O beautiful deceiver, stay!
Illusion all, yet true, except to time,
The mocking mime:
   Of all that happens thou canst change the day!

Why are her eyeballs hid,
Why downcast is their lid?
Her cheek is smarting with a lover's tear.
   Her lips the kiss retain,
The ring he bade her wear
   Her finger takes again.
Her glance he fails to find:
She dares not look, lest it betray her mind.
   Oft while she listens to his tale,
She feels her hand to touch the ring he gave,
The blush to save:
   Does it desert her finger wan and pale?

Heard was the tinkling bell
Before the curtain fell.
The hidden chorus sang the warning strain
   But not the sense to reach;
It died away again,
   But not the sense to teach.
O penalty of sleep,
To smile in sorrow and in joy to weep!
   And yet, O cold deceiver, stay!
Illusion all, but true the mocking mime,
Except to time:
   Of all that happens thou canst change the day!

VALCLUSA.

When sleep at length expires,
The dream her eye attires
And brings her lover with her to the light.
   But soon his image flies
The rapture of her sight,
   And in her presence dies.
Before her senses play
The mists in which his phantom melts away.
   One scream, and she is heard no more;
Unconscious left, and snatched beyond the scope
Of one frail hope;
   Nor all the angel's love can sense restore.

XI.

VALCLUSA.

STRANGE are all toils, most strange the toils of breath
To suck in being or succumb to death!
The weeds of thought about each other twin'd
That grow as on a common o'er the mind,
Are by a breeze sustained, a breath of air,
And this cut off no art can life repair.
Precarious being, spark that scarce belongs
To those in whom its world of passion throngs.
Man's days are few and yet how sad to some;
What should be present always yet to come.
Man living so, his life too soon begins;
What later is to be too late he wins.
Better like us ere birth to lag behind
Till all is fitted to delight the mind.

CHORUS.

Shall fate a passage shape
That leaves her no escape;
Deathless is she that pain may yet endure?
   A sickness hourly grows,
That time may reach the cure
   No sudden art bestows.
Ah! less than mortal prize
Is that which sorrow would immortalise!
   What can avail the boon unblest
If the eternal opens to begin
With deadly sin?
   While distance hides the city of her rest!

But justice is to be:
Stamped is the hard decree,
Nor deem the law inequitable still
   When she, whom it requites,
Is chosen to fulfil
   Its all-abhorrent rites.
Love now its fealty keeps,
Though on the gem exhausted passion sleeps.
   Far from her thoughts is hate removed:
Its shape not yet has argued with her eyes
Its heresies;
   It points no poniard at the heart she loved.

O smile of truth, betray'd,
How is thy loss repaid ?
Whence comes new virtue, whence its fresh delight?
  In vain the soul shall fast,
For deeper sinks the blight,
  The farther from the past!
The memory of sin
Is nursed by famished thoughts that droop within,
  And Heaven in vain the lost deplores :
Not all the coffered treasure of her grace
A resting-place
  Provides, or fallen innocence restores.

VALCLUSA.

Daphne had seen and wept
The joys of her who slept.
She marked the smile disporting on the lip;
  Beheld the bosom move,
With sudden heave and dip
  In wantonness of love;
And with her softer sigh
Strove to appease a jealous power on high.
  Though levity on slumber gain,
Should there be due a debt of penitence
Heaven takes offence :
  For stolen joy has its allotted pain.

Now trance has boundless sway;
Madeline it bears away
To share the thoughtless void. No rest she takes,
    But lingers low and faint;
Nor night nor day she wakes.
    Heard is her mournful plaint
At every breath she plies,
To jar the cord of life until she dies!
    From moan to moan the cruel spell
Escorts her drowsy feelings as they move
To strains of love,
    And in Æolian sighs to passion swell.

Her arms of ease despoiled,
Now on her bosom coiled,
Now tossed about in turn from side to side,
    Like music softly rove:
Their troubles they divide,
    Then meet again in love.
Her gilded tresses blend;
In wild delirium on her breast descend
    To hide from shame its ravished lot!
The wasted hands no more, with nimble grasp,
Those riches clasp:
    As emblems of despair their charms forgot.

In trance from day to day
Her sacred body lay.
The eyes with fringing lash to heaven upturned,
   In lifeless beauty stare;
But, like two lamps unburned,
   No ray with her they share,
And only ask the light,
With blind appeal, to give them back their sight.
   Orbs unobservant, that appear
On leave of absence, while the groping mind
No path can find
   Through the blue rainbow of their parting tear.

The pendule of the will
Now vibrates now hangs still,
Swayed like an incense, whose ecstatic fire
   Her smothered soul devours:
Though still her fond desire
   Its plaintive note outpours,
In moans subdued and slow
Which murmur back her sorrow as they flow.
   Not conscious, her sweet body cries
For yet a little love in its distress;
Her wretchedness
   Shrill to all hearts, benumbing to all eyes.

CHORUS.

Has mercy, like the sky,
For all one same reply?
One round of good that bends on none in vain,
    But deigns to none a choice,
Though rueful he complain,
    Though hopeful he rejoice!
As well were it to plead
Along the twilight pomp that shades the dead,
    As now of heaven a boon implore
For her who launched upon the angered tide
Must there abide
    The better morrow yet for her in store.

XII.

VALCLUSA.

FROM mountain chain, snow-capped, to mountain
 chain,
The encampment floats above the sacred plain.
But now the standard droops in listless folds,
Though every tent a watchful spirit holds:
Hid in its azure plaits the signal star
More sad in truce than spirit-stirring war.

Now by the mountain side,
Where thoughts like waters glide,
Sits Daphne in a lustrous tissue draped,
 Knotted at either arm.
In waving beauty shaped,
 It consecrates the charm
While down her breast it gleams,
And circles to her lap in fulgent streams.

There on the eddying garment rests
A woman's elbow, in its flood immersed,
Ere thence dispersed
   Its floating fold the parted knees invests.

Her nude right arm ascends
And o'er the wretched bends
Whose cheek the open palm its shadow yields:
   An attitude divine!
Her love the helpless shields
   Who leans on her supine,
With rounded shoulder shelved
Upon the pliant breast where it had delved.
   Recumbent in the sultry shade,
Madeline at length enjoys, in languid grace,
A resting-place;
   Her truce awhile with feeble Nature made.

The kiss still haunts her lip
Its ecstasy to sip,
And on voluptuous beauty hold a feast.
   Yet love might turn to hate
Within a calmer breast,
   The past to expiate.
What in that face so dear
Whispers to Daphne, now, the thrilling fear?

Can love the longing lips divide,
The listless features govern with its spell,
And yet foretel
    The subtlety of hate, the lull of pride?

But though of placid mood,
The Furies round her brood;
And, when she sleeps, they sleep beside their prey;
    And when she dreams, her dream
They urge her to obey,
    With rusted looks that gleam :
Like hounds before the chase,
Their instincts whetted for the hungry race.
    To Daphne's eyes not hard to prove,
For love ranks foremost of prophetic powers,
What tempest lowers,
    Held in the net necessity had wove.

How gentle is she now!
No line disturbs her brow;
Her bosom pendant, like a setting orb,
    Its throb from anger weans,
Thoughts holier to absorb.
    On peace her spirit leans
Encircled by its wings,
Like the paternal planet by its rings.

Weak through affliction, in the bliss
Of sympathy she revels like a dove
Beside its love:
   And oft her placid cheek receives a kiss.

But in the distance brood
Thoughts not to be withstood,
   That to the virgin wound untimely haste.
  Is love or hate most dear
Where sweet affections waste?
   The mellow fruits they bear
From one same bough may drip
Their luscious poison on the thirsting lip.
  Hid from her vision, as she lies,
Ascend high towers, her lover's ancient hold,
With turrets bold,
   That furnish grandeur to the modest skies.

The robe that round her flows
Is stirred like drifted snows;
Its restless waves her marble figure drape,
  And all its charms express,
In ever-changing shape,
  To zephyrs that caress
Her limbs, and lay them bare,
And all their grace and loveliness declare.

Madeline.

 Nor modesty itself could chide
The soft enchanters as they past her breathe,
And beauty wreathe
 In rippling forms that ever onward glide.

Breezes from yonder tower,
Loosed by the avenging power,
Her senses hurry, and a dread impart.
 In tremor she beholds
Her fluttering raiment start
 In ribbed and bristled folds.
Its texture close and fine
With broidery sweeps the bosom's heaving line,
 Then trickles down as from a wound,
Curdling across the heart as past it steals,
Where it congeals
 In horrid clots her quivering waist around.

Now from her cincture weep,
As limpid waters creep,
The gentle folds that her sweet body bathe,
 Ere coursing to her feet
The nether limbs to swathe.
 What charms the eye to greet!
The modest bosom's slant,
The bended knees, the shoulder petulant.

Can art midst all her marbles show
Ideal orbs that rise like hill on hill
With heaving thrill;
   And vales that with a living vesture glow?

Sounds, as the cadence sweet
When verse and music meet,
Distract her ear; but in her clouded eyes,
   Where lash and shadow play,
A sadness deeper lies
   Than dims their blue array;
A weary look that tells
Of sorrow past, and on new sorrow dwells!
   She lists as Daphne's words express
All that her love can utter save a tear,
And that is near;
   The accessory yet the soul's excess.

" Oft didst thou hear me tell,—
O mark my warning well!—
Ere thou canst cross the purple dome again
   To touch the happy shore,
Exempt from future pain
   And sinned against no more,
To live where angels live,—
The one ordeal yet is to forgive!

But at thine eyes the thought divine
In one sad glance recedes from paradise,
When it might rise
 To catch the glories destined to be thine!"

Words not too mild to chide
The weak one at her side,
Prompted by hope that warbles as it sinks
 Into its own despair!
How human nature shrinks
 From scenes than life more fair!
Madeline saw not the prize,
Held not the hope its worth to realise.
 Her soul as earthly dew was cold.
Glory broke on her, but with jaggèd ray,
And turned away,
 When her despair in Daphne's ear she told:

" How can I want to die
And hie where spirits hie?
Thy tones my senses in their sweetness steep;
 The transports of thy voice
My soul from sinking keep.
 O that I had the choice
To rest as now with thee,
And as I am, thy own to ever be!

Safe by thy side I murmur not;
No wish beyond, if it were mine to choose,
Lest thee I lose:
So blest thy love there is no better lot!

" Sad though my days may be,
Am not I still with thee?
Thou wouldst recal how once my spirit clomb,
   While sleeping by thy side,
To heaven, its living tomb:
   But monsters round me glide
And snatch my hopes away,
And mock my prayer the more I seek to pray.
   They drive my supplications hence,
Combing their fingers through the snaky curls
Their head unfurls,
   And crimson tears shed o'er my penitence."

" Forgive!" the angel's word:
Where thrilled its answering chord?
Heard was its echo as a sad farewell
   To all with love akin.
A fluted ear the knell
   Heard strike and sink within:
To memory it clung
Like ill-timed syllables at random rung.

Madeline.

As oft the drear, autumnal wind
Whistles to ghosts to hear its doleful whine,
On Madeline
The warning fell, and died within her mind.

In half eclipse her gaze
Veiled by the filmy haze,
Moves in its transit, as a glowworm meek.
   Her spirit goes alone
The exiled hope to seek,
   That has already gone.
Still, holding by one ray,—
The last to linger in the wake of day,—
   She turns her captive look about
That wanders like a trouble of the brain
In search of pain,
   Before her dimmest light, despair, goes out.

With Madeline's sinking sun
The angel's course had run:
What thence befel was like departing day.
   So Daphne drooped in night,
And gave her soul away
   To hers that took its flight.
Was her sad sister gone?
Yet not to wake and say she died alone!

But Madeline first the death-watch broke:
A moan was heard, the fire within her burned,
Her pangs returned;
   The old despair once more the angel woke.

In Madeline's mind she saw
A dull, unringing flaw:
Muffled the once ecstatic note of wo!
   In sullen doubt and dread,
With looks that come and go,
   The angel's soul she read.
So that ill-fated love
Receding through the past had yet to rove,
   And heavenly consolation spurn!
Must vengeance, now at large, full length recoil,
Balked of its spoil,
   And still unsated on the avenger turn?

CHORUS.

O that a milder fate
The past might expiate,
And her unholy penance ever cease!
   Alas, the hate that clings
No penance can appease
   But human offerings!
These work a spell on pain
When all appeal to justice is in vain.

Fate then assumes the single sway,
Lest the tried soul, to utmost fury wrought,
Rend thought from thought,
And on itself the debt of vengeance pay.

VALCLUSA.

Sleep, saucy, hovering drone,
Can sceptred soul dethrone
And rifle of its thought, ephemeral flower
    That loves the drowsy wing,
And welcomes it to power,
    Oblivion though it bring.
Yet to the soul deposed
Clear sight, mysterious gift, may be disclosed
    To filch unwary thoughts that stray
In other souls, and gambol in disguise,
Nor fear surprise ;
    But deem all hid their solitary way.

Clear sight on Daphne fell,
The workings of the spell
Transporting, as in trance, her senses keen
    To Madeline's inmost mind ;
To gaze on worlds unseen
    With eyes else stony blind,
And secrets to descry
Wondrous as scenes revealed in prophecy.

O sleep, thy wave, at best to tire,
Breaks in successive dreams with night-long zeal,
For woe for weal;
   But now is tipped with phosphorescent fire!

Daphne that sleep conjures,
Daphne that sleep endures
Whose hollow eyes survive to gaze at fate,
   The darkness to illume,
The madness penetrate;
   The misery to exhume
Within the spirit's seat;
To watch the wail its monody repeat.
   For sympathy, divinely grand,
Can bridge ethereal ocean and escort,
From port to port,
   The visionary sleeper by the hand.

To that ordeal set
Daphne her trial met :
The cup of sorrow crossed her ruby lip;
   The dregs of earth she drained!
Who can that chalice sip
   By its contents unstained ?
Yet did she drink it dry,
To pledge her soul to human charity,

To sink into the bitter death:
Her glazing eyes dilated as they face,
In chill embrace,
    The sharp concussion of its rimy breath.

Where fury touched its prime,
Not conscious of its crime,
Her eyes in patient wonder fix their sight;
    Like serpents on their prey
On Madeline they alight.
    They see the will obey,
Not long to oscillate,
The final cast that dooms her soul to hate.
    They see with horror's bristled stare
In angry shade the orb of conscience sweep
The spirit's deep,
    And with the passion in its triumph share.

Nor is her view confin'd
To the tormented mind,
Uttering as it ferments a tongue of flame.
    She sees what gestures dire
Distort the sufferer's frame,
    And register its ire.
Madeline in frantic rage
Enacts these antics on a holy stage,

An angel sleeping in her room.
In its unbridled fires her soul finds vent,
On murder bent;
    Led surely on to meet her settled doom.

Her hand a poniard holds
Hid in the restless folds
That from the cincture at her waist descend,
    To rustle as they flow;
And with her fury blend;
    And with her phrensy glow.
Lit by the vengeful mind,
Their glare is tossed and maddened by the wind.
    The flash, with scintillating rays,
Around her robe, asbestos-woven, sweeps;
And as it creeps
    To her bright fingers, on the weapon plays.

From Daphne's pallid lid,
A full-grown tear had slid,
Her cheek with sorrow's seed to early sow.
    And now the braided tress
In curls begins to flow
    Stirred by the wilderness;
While trickle from each pore
Dew-drops that stain their track with limpid gore.

Sighs spread their fluctuating wings
To call down pity on the present hour,
As they outpour
   The melody of prayer from broken strings.

Her hands are clasped in pain,
A shrill, heart-rending strain
Impinges terror on the startled air.
   Madeline aroused in fright
Beholds her own despair
   The angel's visage blight;
The pangs her heart that rack,
A face divine on her reflecting back.
   Her eyes transfixed in stony fear,
Through horror's mask she gazes on the trance,
Until her glance
   Is clouded over by a frozen tear.

Such anguish well she knows
From her own bosom flows:
And it disarms the rage that gores her brain.
   On Daphne's neck she hangs;
Her love implores again:
   Benumbed her recent pangs.
She wipes away the tears
One sorrow for another sorrow bears,

And in mute agony relates;
Asks, in remorse, the angel to revive;
Once more to live,
    And look upon the one she consecrates!

As from a soul's repose
The angel's eyes unclose.
They open on their morrow; thither led
    Lest present they deplore
The vision that had fled,
    And sleep on earth no more.
Those scenes had they outrun
As fast as shadows dip before the sun.
    Though moth-like scorched those loving eyes,—
Too sentient to endure the world of pain
And life sustain,—
    Foreclosed in darkness were their agonies.

XIII.

VALCLUSA.

So did the Furies in their rage abate,
But left the soul adept though desolate.
Tranquil once more in that too short release,
Madeline regains an interval of peace.
Like the vast ocean struggling fate behaves:
Her course one stream, while intermit the waves.

CHORUS.

Who on the ruffled tides
Before the tempest glides,
No upward gaze to face the polar star
   That yet the bark had saved?
Whose end, now not afar
   Is on the tempest graved?
The bark with fluttering sail
Still scuds along in lonely passion's trail!

Madeline, whom fate all chance denied,
Had struggled as no other strove for love,
Nor rose above
   The vulgar lot to suffer till she died.

She long was drawn from harm;
No unavailing charm
The angel's faith that long the wreck delayed!
   With doom she wrestled on,
   And oft its anger stayed,
      And oft its pity won.
Yet she who keeps her pure
Scarce aids her soul its tortures to endure.
   Sad is the presence of a saint!
Placed in its light is wailed the early sin,
That shrinks within,
   Till self-repression chafes at all restraint.

So time drags on the chain.
The morn comes home again,
The even rests upon the weary globe:
   The sun in spangles gay,
The moon in vestal robe,
   Had each its holiday.
The winds still gently blew,
The groves their laurels wove in wreaths anew.

The rocks frowned o'er the stream untired,
The bard still watched his Daphne not afar,
His true lode-star;
And Madeline's wrong his quenchless anger fired.

VALCLUSA.

Reclining side by side
Two loving hearts divide
One peaceful beat, and share the self-same smile;
   One time in breathing keep;
One dream along defile
   Within the world of sleep:
Like symbols of the mind
Their rosy arms around each other twined.
   In this new sympathetic state
They hold discourse, in question and reply,
And oft say, Why?
   As with closed lids and open hearts they prate.

Each other's words they chase
In aptly chiming pace,
Then long they pause and cut the dream in twain;
   Then, where they parted, meet,
And recommence the strain,
   By absence rendered sweet.
Ideas with trouble fraught
Down in the filmy arms of sleep are caught;

Ideas, by these displaced below,
Uprise and to the level surface speed,
Like floating weed,
   And the translucent margin overflow.

The spirit's ebbing tide
With buoyant thoughts they ride,
And take their pleasure to its listless falls.
   One to another's eyes
A happy scene recals;
   A happy scene replies;
One to another's ears
Invokes a better world, and heaven appears.
   And now their steps the rise ascend:
In prints of angels' feet they run away,
At first in play;
   But stop for breath before their journey's end.

The will on nothing set,
They turn without regret
To give their lips and tongues a faster play,
   That lighter truth resolves;
And all they think they say
As memory revolves:
The future and the past
In novel moulds of mingled feeling cast.

" Once more to choose should it be thine,
Wouldst thou to earth this kindly visit pay?"
The answer, Nay!
　But not with earnest smile although divine.

" Born to diffuse the grace
Of thy celestial race,
Yet truly wouldst thou, man himself to save,
　Revisit earth and me?
To languish by the grave,
　Though brief the term might be,
Then sum up all, above,
In one deep sigh of unrequited love!
　Oh, if to choose once more were thine,
Wouldst thou, indeed, this tristful visit pay?"
The answer, Nay!
　With yet less earnest smile, though more divine.

" Thou who didst pine to know
The pains endured below,
Couldst never more to this sad scene return,
　To taste again of death;
To share the poet's urn,
　To share the poet's wreath!
Let fate the suppliant keep,
And still pursue in waking and in sleep!"

But as the thought o'er slumber crept
The angel turned; in her a jarring note
Its utterance smote,
    And her bruised ear in silent reverie kept.

On her begins to gleam
A dream within a dream.
An unborn slumber strangely felt in sleep
    Lies quickening in the mesh
That drags oblivion's deep.
    Nor came its breathings fresh.
It held her whom she served;
The dagger poised, the heart to vengeance nerved.
    But that blank look which gazer chides
Ruled in the eyeball; as a statue's, bold
As it is cold:
    Madeline in that hereafter which it hides.

And not less harsh a stream
Ran through the other's dream.
Her feet meandered with a pebbly shoal
    Whose waters, seen before,
Were striving for some goal,
    Though beating on its shore.
It was the golden beach
She long had tried, she long had failed to reach.

Madeline.

Then asked she, They who here begin,
Strict to the hour of prayer, the hour of song,
Lost in the throng,
Can they forget the memory of sin?

She paused on that sad thought,
For no response it brought.
Then from the broken theme she tasked discourse
   Up to its babbling spring.
Unguarded was the source,
   Nor thence 'twas hard to wring
A secret safely kept
Till wisdom in the angel's bosom slept.
   " Tell me who dwells in yonder tower!
The restless winds flow thence across my brain
In gusts of pain :
   Who can express the terror of their power !"

Unwary in her rest,
In thrilling tones addrest,
The angel whispers the seducer's name.
   Now twangs the chord of hate:
The hour designed for shame
   Struck by a watchful fate.
Shame, with a sudden rush,
Drowns the fair sleeper in its purple blush.

Silent she lies, her efforts vain
To speak or move; too early or too late,
For on her sate
　An incubus and bound her with a chain.

A lifetime intervenes
With its few chequered scenes;
And these begin, glide on, and touch her prime;
　Take fortune's rapid turns;
All in a flash of time
　That scarce a moment burns.
An age appears its gleam;
The whole past blank relighted by a dream.
　She enters now an hour unborn,
Bursting the future track that fate's decree
Had ruled to be:
　The way untrod and yet for footsteps worn.

After a lapse of time
She utters thus her chime:
" He walks a sea of blood with ruby shore,
　All carmine to the sky.
He sinks to rise no more.
　Will he be let to die?
He drowns as now I gaze:
My eyes look on, intoxicate and glaze.

I must be gone, not idle stand
On these enchanted sands to count the beats
My heart repeats;
The loud reveillé tells the hour at hand!"

At this a trumpet's sound
The angel's heart winds round;
It echoes through her present memory
 To when her life began:
In heaven was its reply.
 The ghosts that slumber span,
Like voidings from the grave,
In terror pass; her soul becomes their slave.
 By their relentless power appalled,
She looks on death, and to its dread event
Her will is bent,
 As one whom fate had conquered and enthralled.

She who had lived to bless,
Gazed on the pitiless,
In anguish clinging to her mortal state.
 Above her stood the Form,
Her heart to immolate
 And scatter in the storm,
To dust her beauty change:
Her grave to be the whirlwind's sunless range.

Yet, as she swooned in sight of Death,
Her eyes saw heaven, not merciless or cold,
Its clouds unfold;
   And in that trance she sighed away her breath.

CHORUS.

Ah, not in wanton mood
She gave up selfish good,
When none had envied her, though rich her store!
   She pined her heart to train
In seats of human lore
   And minister to pain.
Was there not much to learn?
The prize, now won, how hard alas, to earn!
   But through her passport ran the grace
To meet this hour, to triumph at its end
As woman's friend,
   And better than she left, her path retrace.

XIV.

VALCLUSA.

THE trump of doom that Daphne's spirit rends
From her sweet body, and her trouble ends,
Is heard along the camp, where, slumber-bound,
The angels tremble in its piercing sound.
Startled as one, they straightway strike their tents:
It is the close of these divine events.
Accomplished is their task; the word of power
Has visible possession of the hour,
And to his last account has summoned hence,
To expiate in death his deep offence,
Him who knew passion yet no pity knew,
And with his love its human ties withdrew.
As they depart cloud-storms forthwith arise
From hidden seas; the frighted moon surprise.
The blowing mists and their wild shadows fly
Against the clinging colours of the sky,

To now eclipse, now liberate their light:
A scene resembling not the day or night.
At length they rush before the heavenly queen
Who falls behind and is no further seen.

The angel's hour of peace
Saw not the struggle cease,
For it foretold the scarce less sudden close
    Of one yet sadder lot.
Madeline in sleep arose
    Her slumber waking not,
Bound to its purpose still
The work of fate to prosper and fulfil.
    On Madeline's ear unnoticed fell
Those dying moans, her sense towards one event
Omnipotent,
    Held in the grasp of one resistless spell.

Her tongue the silence keeps:
Her voice for ever sleeps;
But her fierce dream the stirring impulse moves,
    With purpose blind and mute,
To act as fate approves,
    And helps to execute.
Low rustlings of a wind
That in ravines remote had lagged behind,

Madeline.

Attend her, mourning, on her path.
Her arm outstretched to grasp the dagger's hilt,
This slave of guilt
    Resigns her footsteps to the weapon's wrath.

The poniard in her hand,
Poised like a fiery brand,
She glides to where it leads; her naked feet
    In safety trace their way:
No obstacle they meet
    Her journey to delay,
While rising like a star
The weapon lights her on her path afar.
    From danger's way she nimbly turns;
Swayed by the winds she overhangs the gap;
Her garments flap;
    But on its destined track her spirit burns.

She leaps from rock to rock
Unconscious of the shock;
Her tender feet by crystals cut and bled!
    She fords the raging flood,
And leaves the ripple red
    With traces of her blood.
She climbs the harrowing steep;
Now up, now down her wary footsteps creep.

Along the brink, whose icy drip
In the abyss a roaring torrent finds,
Her course she winds,
   Nor shuns the glacier in its headlong slip.

Again, her figure frail
The howling gusts assail;
Beside her track the precipice outspread.
   But as in fairy dance
The nymphs on music tread,
   Her well-timed steps advance.
Her magic guide is mute;
More safe to follow than the fulsome flute.
   The very storms whose sudden gush
Thus vent aloud their undiscerning rage,
The fates engage
   To poise her in the scale as past they rush.

Within the thunder's peal,
Her glory to reveal,
She stops, unshaken by the aimless crash.
   She moves another pace
Into the lightning's flash,
   Averting not her face.
Old votaries of fate,
Above her all the waters congregate:

But not on heaven her eyes are bent,
Though there, to devastate the earth again
In ruin's train,
The ancient deluge rears a monument.

And where the lightnings smite
A world of day they write,
Then shut the page of their immortal book.
   They smite upon the rock,
They smite upon the brook,
   The fountains to unlock,
The hill-tops to display;
To show the night the equal of the day.
   The high despotic vault they rive;
They marshal clouds of thunder to advance
And seize the chance
   To plunder heaven of its prerogative.

With heavy fall and bound
Rain sweeps the troubled ground;
The playing waters froth the busy mud
   Where amber-bubbles rush,
And airy vessels scud;
   Their streams the gangway flush.
The leafy vine is riven
And from its moorings down the current driven.

Queen of the storm, the sleeper wends
Along its van, and in the lightning's beam
Conducts her dream.
   Disordered Nature on her rage attends.

Now comes with sphinx-like face
Ineffable in grace,
The ample moon encircled by her spell,—
   Her own by right divine,—
The elements to quell.
   They watch her glory shine.
She seems to bear in state
The secret of inexorable fate.
   Nor she the rising towers conceals,
While Madeline, at the bridge that spans the moat,
In robes that float,
   Walks in the flood of splendour she reveals.

In light and shadow told,
Are there the days of old.
Unwelcome is the stranger at the gate.
   A watch-dog guardant lies
That in unsleeping hate
   With mortal more than vies;
But when in measured grace
The sleeper's fearless steps his threshold pace

'Tis he who feels the mortal dread.
He pours along the under-vaulted way
His hollow bay,
To warn the mighty living through the dead.

When through the gate she flits,
One at the portal sits
Encased in mail and armed with shield and spear.
　As past his eyes she trips
They follow her in fear,
　And silent are his lips.
Others the passage line
And with like awe look on her as divine.
　Along the ranks her poniard's glare
Conveys no threat: but only seen the ghost
That threads the host,—
　She of their solemn muster unaware.

The unclosed doorway leads
To where the banquet spreads;
And on the daïs, gay at the festal hour,
　The guests in knightly grace
The red libation pour,
　Each in his bannered place.
Why does the flowing wine
Congeal like clusters hung upon the vine?

Why pass those looks of horror round?
Pale every face, one pale no more to flush.
They hear the gush,
    The blood that gurgles from a mortal wound.

And in that self-same sleep,
So mystic, wild, and deep,
Madeline returns and by the angel lies.
    Nor has the wound that bled,
Across her heavy eyes
    Its ruby lustre shed.
That sleep, by justice sent
With dreams that ever echoed its intent,
    Had worked for her its ample spoil.
And the seduced, the once seductile maid,
All hate allay'd,
    Resumes her virgin slumber through its toil.

EPILOGUE.

VALCLUSA.

Is she unhappy ? No !
Hers is a hidden wo.
She loves him still, now free of passion's snare.
  So let her conscience lie
Coiled up exempt from care,
  As if uncast the die !
Heaven is at times content
To hide from view what man might else repent,
  Though far removed from his controul :
Whence, in this act, was memory set at rest,
Not to attest
  To deeds committed in the dark of soul.

Urged onward in her fate
To dream her love to hate,
Shall reason blame her in discourses vain,
  With its poor sayings why :

A fester called the brain
  The laws eternal try?
These words the angels spake:
We saw the wave of retribution wake
  With Madeline on its swollen crest,
Pillowed in dream and mounted to disband,
With guided hand,
  An unrelenting sinner to his rest.

Fate was within all change;
Far sweeping was its range;
When Madeline, conscious of her heart's repose,
  By Daphne's side reclined,
Till from that tomb she rose.
  Two souls in death entwined
No more to separate:
Nor long they lay locked up in marble state.
  Then timely rent the mortal seam,
That they at length in purity might vie,
As once they die,
  And leave in sculpture their immortal dream.

One silent day is all
That bears in heaven their pall.
They winter in its sunshine, though its fire
  Warm not their cold remains.

On the funereal pyre,
  Set free all mortal pains,
The relict Slander springs
And consecrates to death his burning wings.
  Reluctant to survive the end!
That none the broken shaft hereafter throw,
Or palsied bow
  Across the ashes of the dead distend.

Unknown to them their sleep,
As unborn Nature deep,
The angel first broke through its solid gloom.
  Her gaze the dawn renewed
Within the sleeper's room,
  When Madeline's breast she strewed
With green-winged budded rose,
Soon like her eyes its petals to unclose.
  And not to greet that joy alone,
Upon a mother's heart, then cold as clay,
A babe she lay,
  Its smiles on her to shower when morrow shone.

The angel early gave
A signal at the grave:
Morn's virgin ray had scarcely crossed the face
  Of her who held her breath

In soft sepulchral grace,
  That figured early death,
When she the trumpet blew,
The bud once plucked in blossom to renew.
  Three angels in advance arise;
They lead the narrow way, to earth unseen
That lies between
  Immortalising forms and paradise.

Their arms each other round,
Those three in one are bound,
And face to face they drag their comely rays
  Along a sunlit sky,
That scarce their path betrays.
  Yet, like a galaxy,
Vast wonders they display;
New heavens create for earths that pass away.
  And ever they reveal fresh charms,
In circling beauty, to each other's love;
And float above
  Linked in the sweetness of each other's arms.

CHORUS.

Faith is the name of one:
In soul the most alone.

A cross her vision fills and unerased
  Within her ever burns:
By her its symbol chased
  On cinerary urns.
No doubt her being chills
That with its raptures all creation fills.
  The elder of this triple throng,
Her eyes as marble dim, and cold her sight
To Nature's light,
  She seems scarce kin to those she dwells among.

Then Hope with beams that dance
Athwart her pearly glance!
As through the leaves the fitful glimmer plies,
  She lights the shades of love
  With sun-drops from her eyes,
    And draws all hearts above.
They who desire to live,
Though fleeting be the wish, in her survive.
  The voice of Nature calls on her
From the round earth, and when she is not near
Is she most dear;
  And all aspire to be her passenger.

And how less dreamy she
The younger of the three!

She envies not, and all her bounty hides
  The more all hearts to move.
She vaunts not, nor she chides,
  For all her words are love.
Charity never fails,
She all outlives and over all prevails.
  And she alone can never die!
With a career and destiny sublime
That outstrips time,
  She lingers ever in eternity.

VALCLUSA.

Their path the pilgrims find,
And with no careworn mind
As when the euthanasia was at hand.
  For films of fancy spun
By the sweet triple band,
  Are into traces run
To drag a load of love;
The web by heavenly machinations wove.
  The gossamer in glistening strings
Drawn out like ray from ray and thought from
    thought,
So finely wrought,
  Waves to and fro on its ethereal wings.

The three, with welcome, greet
The way-worn pilgrims' feet,
And bear them upwards as they pass the knell.
    Burst then was Nature's tie;
But garbs were left to tell
    Of those for once who die.
Their stoles they leave behind,
And in the phosphor clouds their members bind.
    There they abide the frisky team,
Broke in the sun for pilgrims on their way
To distant day,
    Whence earth seems gilded over like a dream.

Soft beads of evening dew
The jointed cords bestrew,
And glisten with an image of a star.
    The loose, tenacious thread
Gets tangled in the car
    Which holds the souls once dead,
Who, through the realm of night,
Take with the laughing babe their rapid flight,
    Bound for the verge of paradise.
They give one look at earth before they move;
One look of love;
    Then, like a wain, in right ascension rise.

PARABLES.

THE LILY OF THE VALLEY.

THERE was a wood, it does not change,
   Not while the thrush pipes through its glades,
And she who did its thickets range
   Has willed her sunbeam to its shades.
There still the lily weaves a net
With bluebell, primrose, violet.

The wood is what it was of old,
   A timber-farm where wild flowers grow.
There woodman's axe is never cold,
   And lays the oaks and beeches low.
But though the hand of man deface,
The lily ever grows in grace.

Of their sweet, loving natures proud
   The stock-doves sojourn in the tree:
With breasts of feathered sky and cloud,
   And notes of soft though tuneless glee,
Hid in the leaves they take a spring,
And crush the stillness with their wing.

The Lily of the Valley.

The wood is deep-boughed, and its glade
    Has ruts of waggon to and fro;
And where the print of wheel is made
    The bracken ventures still to grow;
And where the foot of man may goad,
The ants are toiling with their load.

The wood, so old in other days,
    No longer alters with the year.
The gnarlèd boughs, to Nature's ways
    Inured, their honours mildly bear.
And she who there transfixed her beam,
Is still remembered as a dream.

The wood to her was the old wood,
    The same as in her father's time;
Nor with their sooths and sayings good
    The dead told of its youth or prime.
The hollow trunks were hollow then,
And honoured like the bones of men.

There like nine brethren, Nature's own,
    Nine trees within a circle stand,
And to a temple's shape have grown,
    Each trunk a column tall and grand.
And, near, a raven-oak outspreads
A dome that to the ether leads.

'Mid these, while on the earth at play,
   She the true beam of living spring,
And playmate of the lily's ray,
   Learnt of the piping thrush to sing.
The lily's leaves were then her nest,
Its buds half-nestled in her breast.

And she whose beam was lily-bright
   'Neath brakes without a sky above,
A primrose thought a holy sight:
   Loveless itself it taught her love.
It was her welcome to the bowers,
And lured her fingers to its flowers.

Not to her eyes was Nature's age
   In gnarled and hollow shapes revealed:
The buds and leaflets stamped her page,
   And all that Death could say concealed.
To gnarled and hollow Nature cold,
She had not caught the sense of old.

When asked her name, the child so pale,
   By folk who gossiped thereabout,
She answered: Lily of the Vale,
   With looks that gave a sweetness out.
But on her eyes now dew-drops shed
Their early tribute to the dead.

Alas, her parents came to die,
   Nor was she then too young to weep.
Through all the wood was heard her cry;
   At last with sobs she fell asleep.
Changed in that slumber was her beam;
Old was the import of her dream.

The lilies in their nest had died,
   Violets were closed, their petals dim,
The bracken-stalk was parched and dried,
   The rose she loved, no more was prim.
All her first joys were at an end
To let her soul its scale ascend.

While on the moss she lay asleep
   She saw each gnarled and hollow form:
The riven branches seemed to creep,
   Loosed was their long-enchanted storm.
The raven-oak, a tree she loved,
Through all her soul in ruin moved.

The oak oft seen by her before
   And heeded not as weird and bald,
Was laid up in her memory's store
   Too faint and pale to be recalled,
Till tutoring sorrow should impress
The lesson of her first distress.

The Lily of the Valley.

She dreamed that on the oak old áge
    Leant with a father's loving mind,
And looked upon his heritage;
    The child his son had left behind.
Old was she now, for she could see
A father aged like the tree.

As flowers her eager heart had fired
    With love for things of lighter cast,
This vision in her soul inspired
    Affection for the things that last:
The sire by age and trouble spent,
The tree by winds and lightnings rent.

Sleep left her eyes, but fixed them still,
    For yet the oak her vision kept.
Her open eyes its wonders fill
    As when across its shades she slept.
She looks about the sire to see:
His form no more leant on the tree.

Forthwith she to the cottage ran,
    To catch the sire in his retreat,
And there she found the agèd man
    Too quiet to have left his seat.
And then a keener sense awoke
Than to her soul in visions spoke.

He tells her how the raven reared
    Her young upon the leafy crest;
How now the oak by lightning seared
    Affords no shelter for a nest.
With this her simple thoughts he led
To how the bird the prophet fed.

So when the sire, so old and poor,
    Had failed to earn his daily bread,
She longed to see within his door
    The frugal supper still outspread,
And prayed the raven in her need
To do again the loving deed.

Through every grove she poured her lay,
    This drooping Lily of the Vale;
As through the brakes she took her way
    She told the thrush her touching tale,
And bade it in her service press
The bird that waits on man's distress.

So, like a creature on the wing,
    She spoke her griefs to all she met.
The thrush had taught her how to sing,
    And to his note her song she set.
He was the charmer of the grove,
And to his ear she pledged her love.

The thrush who heard his native strain,
  Its burden deemed a lover's joy,
And so he led his feathered train
  To listen to the sweet decoy;
To her who bade the raven come
Again to its forgotten home.

Meantime the sire from day to day
  Found work too hard for sinking age,
And he earned but a scanty pay
  To keep him and his heritage.
He soon fell sick upon his bed,
Nor by the raven was he fed.

Through brake and bush the orphan flew;
  Beyond the wood there lay the field.
Than this no way she further knew,
  Yet did not to misgivings yield.
She looked at heaven and saw its scope,
Taught by her mother where to hope.

And then she to her mother said:
  " Can God the pretty raven spare?
For grandsire lies upon his bed,
  And has not earned his daily fare.
All father's work he leaves undone,
And says, I soon shall be alone."

She took the road, and seemed to tread
    The buoyant air that past her blew.
She cast her looks about in dread,
    As on the unknown path she flew.
She stopped and gazed around in fear,
For no one, not a soul, was near.

And then she to her father said :
    " Can God the pretty raven spare?
For grandsire lies upon his bed,
    And has not earned his daily fare.
He leaves the work you left undone,
And says, I soon shall be alone."

Her slack'ning pace now plainly told
    The path was long for timid feet.
She felt her heart no longer bold :
    Oft she looked back the wood to greet.
Her wood from sight a moment gone
She felt herself indeed alone.

She stood where hills and valleys blend ;
    One struggle more and heaven was nigh.
Beyond where fields and woods ascend,
    She saw a mansion up on high.
Can it be there the lady lives
Who to the poor her plenty gives?

"Could I," said Lily, "see her face
    She would the orphan's prayer sustain;
Could I but reach her heavenly place
    And meet my mother once again,
Then should I daily succour find,
And drop the burden from my mind."

She looked till in her hopeful soul
    She saw the sight she would obtain;
And so to fancy gave controul,
    She thought the lady looked again.
Through sashes in the stately pile,
She thought she saw a human smile.

And then she to the lady said:
    "Can God the pretty raven spare?
For grandsire lies upon his bed,
    And has not earned his daily fare.
All father's work he leaves undone,
And says, I soon shall be alone."

The mansion stood against the sun:
    There long she looked for her reply.
The ball of fire its course had run,
    And filled with red the western sky.
The twilight brought the shades of night;
    She turned her troubled steps for flight.

She must return, it was too late
    To reach that mansion in the air,
Nor can she all her tale relate
    Though still she sees the lady fair.
But all her little hope had fled :
With fainting steps she homeward sped.

First slowly, then with swifter pace
    She outran terror at her heels,
As if to win with death the race,
    Whose shroud now brushing by she feels.
She starts at every rugged bank,
For with the sun her spirit sank.

The orb yet vast beyond the height,
    Had set more early in the wood ;
But still it gave her half its light,
    Her share of its abundant good.
It left its sinking wick to burn ;
The gleam sufficed for her return.

She spied her cot, O vision sweet ;
    A rushlight through the lattice flamed,
And threw its splendour at her feet,
    As it the grudging twilight shamed.
Through diamond panes a glimpse to snatch
She held her finger on the latch.

No sound, no breath she heard above,
    Where grandsire in the garret lay.
A man in black, with looks of love,
    " Poor little orphan," seemed to say.
His was the curate's humble place,
And well he loved sweet Lily's face.

" Where hast thou been, my darling maid?
    Reply to one who likes thee well."
" To warble to the birds," she said;
    " The raven all my wants to tell.
I sang to them their pretty note,
Oft heard and learned at last by rote."

" Why call the raven to thy door,
    Thy little heart's distress to share?"
" Because," said she, " my sire is poor,
    And has not earned his daily fare.
All father's work he leaves undone,
And says, I soon shall be alone."

" To kiss thee, child, he would have stay'd,
    For oft he called thee to his side.
Where didst thou wander, little maid?"
    " I went across the world so wide.
I looked at heaven and saw its scope,
Taught by my mother there to hope.

" I looked at mother in the sky :
    She taught me there my wants to tell ;
I looked at father standing by,
    For both among the happy dwell ;
I prayed and asked with heart of care,
Can God the pretty raven spare ?

" Then I came nigh a stately pile,
    Where those who ask seek not in vain.
I looked, and saw a human smile,
    And thought the lady looked again.
Through sashes I beheld her face,
And then I knew her heavenly place."

" Why for thy sire seek bread alone ?"
    Then said the friend of human kind ;
" He needs it not, for he is gone ;
    His utmost wants has God divin'd.
He now partakes his father's love,
And with thy parents is above."

" Has then the lady, she who gives
    Her food and raiment to the poor,
And in the heavenly mansion lives,
    Called him up yonder to her door ?
She saw the Lily of the Vale,
And hearkened as I told my tale !

"I sought, and in my hopeful mind
  Beheld the sight I would obtain.
God said that those who seek shall find;
  On me the lady looked again.
Within the sash of yonder pile,
I thought I saw a human smile.

" So then I to the lady said :
  ' Can God the pretty raven spare ?
For grandsire lies upon his bed,
  And has not earned his daily fare.
All father's work he leaves undone,
And says, I soon shall be alone.' "

" Thou shalt not be alone, my child ;
  Thy griefs the righteous lady hears :
She loves a spirit undefil'd ;
  Her heart is open to thy tears.
Thy father's work at last is done,
And thou shalt never be alone."

THE DEADLY NIGHTSHADE.

There was a haunt, it does not change,
   Not while the fiend its path invades:
And he who did its alleys range
   Has willed his penance to its shades.
There still the nightshade breathes its pest
On fallen spirits not at rest.

The haunt is what it was of yore,
   Home of the vile who justice fly:
The voice of Nature heard no more
   Where guilty men seek sanctuary,
And crimes like months afresh appear;
Ere one runs out another near.

A haunt where all in common share
   The sleepless hour, the murderous toil;
Where Death on all has set his stare
   To mock their gain and grasp their spoil,
Their doings soon or late to stop
Upon the old-appointed drop.

The Deadly Nightshade.   141

A charnel that may beauty hide—
  The frantic woman who has gamed
And lost young Nature's virgin pride,
  Who falls to guard the door unshamed:
Unveiled the blemish of her face,
Once passed the moan of her disgrace.

That virgin wreck cast on the beach
  And part recovered, many share;
In her one joy of being reach,
  Until her womb gives up its care,
And innocence its visit pays
To coax her back to virtue's ways.

A theme more sad in evil dwells
  Than trouble from the bosom wrings;
Its fruits the mother's life foretels
  Ere at the breast an infant clings:
True to the meaning of its name,
Its cradle still the lap of shame.

A sadder theme in evil dwells
  Than pain and penury supply;
And wide its scope, for it foretels
  An ever weeping progeny,
A brotherhood whose awful chief
Is sin, the ancestor of grief.

Where only shadows rise and set,
   And love at morn awakens not,
A child of woe his being met,
   His nature noble base his lot.
For whence the mother draws her pains
The new-born soul its part obtains.

That mother looked into the gloom
   As he drew in his early breath;
She only conscious of his doom:
   On one side life another death!
Such was the portion that befel
A little angel born in hell.

His place of birth the heavens deplored,
   No trees, no brooks, no meadows seen:
But still his heart the skies adored
   Before he saw the fields were green.
But born in broils, in squalor bred,
How knew his soul to where it led?

Then many hands the infant train
   With sobs to shed the gushing tear;
To grow a prodigy of pain
   That gentle natures pay to hear.
And many listened and bestowed;
For younger tears had never flowed.

The Deadly Nightshade.

Held at his mother's hand he hung
   A broken spray with misery's drip,
And often to the ground he clung
   His passion bursting at his lip.
Dragged at her arm along the stones,
His feet were tender to the bones.

Her eyes of prey like fangs she laid
   On all who gave a hurried look.
She asked the kind to render aid,
   Nor paused till she their money took.
Now for the burning cup she craves,
And now the deadly potion braves.

With spreading nostril, eyes of flame,
   In front the shrine of death she stands,
The infant by her, sick and lame,
   The lava trembling in her hands.
She drinks the fire, with rapture frowns;
And so the fiend of sorrow drowns.

Is this Dorado that it yields
   A golden harvest to the state?
A pious nation reaps those fields,
   But buries there the profligate.
Why then the meagre fine compel,
Or shut the drunkard in a cell?

Locked up, in prison left to rage,
  A martyr burned in inward fires,
Hope is not present to assuage
  The anguish of her fierce desires.
Such was the mother that befel
An angel born and bred in hell.

Not far away from infancy—
  Through weary time a single stage,
The live-long years that hustled by
  Had left him still of tender age,
When from the frequent blow he fled
Outside the doors to make his bed.

Where odours wandered, dank and foul,
  Through crowded streets and dwellings lone,
For days his prickling footsteps prowl;
  His wants, not many, asked by none:
New all the roads he hourly crossed,
Not lost his way, himself not lost.

When hunger came he begged for bread,
  But only of the stinted few:
Not bold enough to raise his head
  Except to those who famine knew.
Want, cried he, cannot want deny!
It has a face of charity.

The Deadly Nightshade.

And now he glides into a den
   Up whose dusk path a shudder flew,
And asks for bread of famished men
   Whose strength no plenty could renew.
Yet with what startling oaths they rave,
And bid him run his neck to save.

Still to the poor is his appeal,
   But all his meek petition spurn :
Some bid him be a man and steal ;
   Some bid him hang before his turn.
Among so many hearts to die,
And be the hangman's legacy!

O what harsh will, what last bequest
   Affiliates his soul on crime?
Ah! could he eat and be at rest,
   And not his hands with theft begrime!
Is this man's law, a wrath to pour
On generations three and four?

He sleeps, but in delirious fear
   Feels his dark mother's shadow coil
About his visions; ever near
   The welcome state of rest to foil.
For then he felt a hope benign,
In halo set its blessed sign.

The hope benign in halo set
   Partakes of hunger at his side:
The shadow wrestles with it yet,
   But cannot all its beauty hide,
That with the young in trouble stays:
All but the starving pang allays.

Then did he long for once to taste
   The reeking viands, as their smell
From cellar gratings ran to waste,
   In gusts that sicken and repel.
Like Beauty with a rose regaled,
The grateful vapours he inhaled.

So, oft a-hungered has he stood,
   And yarn of fasting fancy spun,
As wistfully he watched the food
   With one foot out away to run,
Lest questioned be his only right
To revel in the goodly sight.

Lest justice should detect within
   A blot no human eye could see,
He dragged his rags about his skin
   To hide from view his pedigree.
He deemed himself a thief by law
Who stole ere yet the light he saw

His theft, the infancy of crime,
  Was but a sombre glance to steal,
While outside shops he spent his time
  In vain imaginings to deal,
With looks of awe to speculate
On all things good, while others ate.

No better school his eyes to guide,
  He lingers by some savoury mass,
And watches mouths that open wide,
  And sees them eating through the glass.
Oft his own lips he opes and shuts;
With sympathy his fancy gluts.

Yet he begs not, but in a trance
  Admires the scene where numbers throng;
And if on him descends a glance
  He is abashed and slinks along;
Nor cares he more, the spell once broke,
Scenes of false plenty to invoke.

The man of charity beholds
  The vagrant with a pent-up grief;
And, often as he stops and scolds,
  Abstains from giving him relief,
So sad to see the idle thrive
And on another's earnings live.

Then is the child, this chosen seed,
   Picked out by fate to sweep the streets:
When some bethink them of his need,
   Though scant the recompense he meets.
At times he walks upon his head:
A form of prayer for daily bread.

There is a prayer whose word devout
   On king and queen a blessing calls:
In it the beggar is left out
   Till he has reached the prison walls,
The palace of the reprobate—
For crimes not sanctioned by the state.

As, true to force, the magnet bar
   Towards its dark polar sea must tend,
As, true to force, the falling star
   Unhelped, must to the mire descend,
So must the angel born in hell
Like these obey the crushing spell.

IMMORTALITY.

Grey locks, the banner of the wise;
   Their pride discharged by bleaching age;
Inscribed with worn-out destinies,
   With battle's sign, without its rage;
The dregs of earth from them effaced,
And Time's pale hand upon them traced.

Grey eyes that look their evening dreams,
   A glittering memory unspoke;
Wan cheeks, that bear the many seams
   Of trouble's shock and ending stroke,
On which fixed pallor waits the call
Well-known to summon one and all.

A man who mused till he was aged,
   Who Nature's eye at last outstared;
In science deemed occult engaged
   Till he had Nature's bosom bared;
A man who saw into the lies
Of all forbidden mysteries.

A man of love, superfluous dower!
   For all around who pleasure wills,
Himself a martyr to the power
   That only bursts the heart it fills!
That scales for nought emotion's height
Crushed through its own returning might.

A man of heart and thought so matched
   That they went on as two in one,
For heart and thought each other watched,
   And ever asked what each had done.
A common end they sought and served,
And never from their purpose swerved.

A man whom fancy, too, endowed
   With some divinity of mind.
To heart and thought this fancy bowed,
   Though hard its flow to stem and bind.
Oft it would wash the universe,
And with an ebb again disperse.

Such was he, but for trial's sake
   He bore these marks of finer clay
The sunless half of life to take
   And in the shadow pass away.
But though rejected, his own kind
Preserved the words he left behind.

Generous was made this soul, and yet
    To be the poorest of his race;
Ambition in this soul was set,
    Yet shut its gates were on his face.
Vain was his hope the goal to win:
The end on earth was, to begin.

And so he drifted on to age,
    His genius ripe without success.
Then he began his life to gauge,
    And measure out its wilderness.
Then did the desert hear his sigh
And bid him speak as death was nigh.

He asked it why it was his lot
    To till those fields of arid sand;
The purpose of his toils forgot
    And vain the cunning of his hand.
Why had the faculty divine
Been let to burn but never shine?

He asked it why a mortal phase
    So fair had missed the click of fame;
Why Nature rather should erase
    Her work than sanctify his name?
The desert's sigh for answer bore:
These things shall trouble thee no more.

And then, alone in soul, he turned
  His thought and heart to earth again.
The light of reason in him burned
  To gild the meaning of his pain;
And, like a ray from heaven that shot,
It broke the secret of his lot.

Now two opposing mirrors glow,
  The Future opposite the Past,
And image after image show
  While either way his eyes are cast.
On every hand the endless shines,
And this strange man its truth divines.

His Past as one long presence glares,
  In it he lives his life again
To glory in his former cares.
  He finds not one that was in vain!
On their bright gallery intent,
His conscience gives its last assent.

Not all, for lo! the vista thrown
  Upon his Future, fills all time:
His life is still to be his own!
  And, in his destiny sublime,
He learns that all his trials came
To turn past days to others' shame.

Immortality.

The Past he saw was not for fame,
  The tuneless clatter of an age:
But for the contest when a name
  Is wanted on the eternal page.
His life was done, but left its fire
In living glory to expire.

Not to enjoy a fame below
  That soon descends into the Past,
But to partake the coming show:
  With all Futurity to last,
Was work of genius to ascend,
And be a touchstone to the end.

To him is given the blended whole;
  To him both vistas are revealed;
They meet in him from either pole,
  So bright that nothing is concealed.
Future and Past before him bared
Are by the man of fate compared.

The Future to his vision clings,
  He looks with an adoring sense,
For though a life once sad he brings
  It is a life of innocence.
To native joys his soul awakes,
And pain his memory forsakes.

Each image more distinct and clear
  Grows in his mind as time revolves,
And as the objects gather near,
  Itself the wondrous problem solves,
For every former foe his state
Exhibits to the man of fate.

The faces that he knew of old
  Across the Future's mirror drift,
Their purpose blindly they unfold,
  That he may mind and motive sift.
The heart holds still its poisoned jet,
The lip is still with honey wet!

The faces try his sight to shun
  Transformed to hideous teeth that gnash;
All from his hated presence run
  With lengthened ears moved towards the lash,
As if his former words were sent
To be their future punishment.

At their own memory they start
To yet, perforce, his pleadings spurn
Till terror-smit their senses part
  And in a maze to earth return.
Still poverty and genius plead,
But speak the language of the dead!

Immortality. 155

So more in wonder than dismay,
   He finds that all who cursed his life,
Are grooved within one selfish way,
   To meet again in endless strife,
While at each step they feel a shock;
The man of fate their stumbling-block.

Not theirs to suffer for their kind,
   To help the sick, the naked clothe;
They saw the touchstone, and were blind;
   They failed the heart and thought to soothe.
These he beholds accursed and smit,
As from his claims they strive to flit.

But to identify their race
   Into the past he turned amazed.
He there perceived each self-same face
   From him averted as he gazed.
To meet these heirs of all his pain,
Almost revives his grief again.

Such was the life of this strange man,
   Such was the meaning of its end.
And it was a consistent plan
   Thus first its value to defend,
Then for a term its virtues nurse
And through their fruits the worthless curse.

His triumph this, that in his hand
    He finds the brazen trump of fame,
Mouthpiece of an immortal band
    Whose shrillness starts the dead to shame,
Lest in their sloth they ever rust,
Soul unto soul, dust unto dust.

So that one man has now command
    The high-born spirits' game to fight,
And over myriads take his stand
    New ages calling into light.
To nature true, not false to art,
So did that man enact his part.

OLD SOULS.

THE world, not hushed, yet lay in trance;
    It saw the future in its van,
It drew its riches in advance,
    To meet the unfelt wants of man;
But length of days, untimely sped,
Left its account unaudited.

The sun untired still rose and set,
    Nor swerved an instant from its beat;
It had not lost a moment yet,
    Nor used in vain its light or heat;
But, in his trance, from when it rose
To when it sank, man craved repose.

A light that once had gone before
    Was reached, despised, and left behind:
The heart was rotting to the core
    Locked in the slumbers of the mind,
Nor beat of drum, nor sound of fife,
Could rouse it to a sense of life.

Old Souls.

A cry was heard, intoned and slow,
    Of one who had no wares to vend:
His words were gentle, dull, and low,
    And he called out, Old souls to mend!
He peddled on from door to door,
And looked not up to rich or poor.

His step kept on as if in pace
    With some old timepiece in his head,
Nor ever did its way retrace,
    Nor right nor left turned he his tread,
But uttered still his tinker's cry
To din the ears of passers-by.

So well was known the olden cry
    Few heeded what the tinker spake,
Though here and there on passers-by
    A sudden hold it seemed to take.
But these had not the time to stay;
And it would do some other day.

Still on his way the tinker wends
    Though jobs be far between and few;
But here and there a soul he mends
    And makes it look as good as new.
Once set to work and fairly hired,
His dull old hammer seems inspired.

Over the task his features glow;
He knocks away the rusty flakes.
  A spark flies off at every blow;
At every rap new life awakes.
The soul once cleansed of outer sins,
His subtle handicraft begins.

Like iron unannealed and rough
  The soul is plunged into the blast:
To temper it, however tough,
  'Tis next in holy water cast.
Then on the anvil it receives
The nimblest stroke the tinker gives.

The tinker's task is at an end:
  Stamped was the cross by that last blow.
Again his cry, Old souls to mend!
  Is heard in accents dull and low.
He pauses not to seek his pay,
That too will do another day.

One stops and says, This soul of mine
  Has been a tidy piece of ware,
But rust and rot in it combine,
  And now corruption lays it bare.
Give it a look; there was a day
When it the morning hymn could say.

The tinker looks into his eye
    And there detects besetting sin,
The decent old-established lie
    That creeps through all the chinks within.
Lank are its tendrils, thick its shoots,
And like a worm's nest coil the roots.

Its flowers a deadly berry bear,
    Whose pip well-tended from the pod
Had grown in beauty with the year,
    Like deodara drawn to God;
Not as the dank and curly brake
That sucks up venom for the snake.

The tinker takes the weed in tow,
    And roots it out with tooth and nail;
His labour patient to bestow
    Lest like the herd of men he fail.
How best to extirpate the weed,
Has grown with him into a creed.

His tack is steady, slow and sure:
    He plucks it out, despite the howl,
With gentle hand and look demure,
    As cunning maiden draws a fowl.
He knows the job he is about,
And pulls till all the lie is out.

"Now steadfastly regard the man
  Who wrought your cure of rust and rot;
You saw him ere the work began:
  Is he the same or is he not?
You saw the tinker, now behold
The Envoy of a God of old."

This said, he on the forehead stamps
  The downward stroke and one across,
Then straight upon his way he tramps;
  His time for profit not for loss;
His task no sooner at an end
That out he cries, Old souls to mend!

As night comes on he enters doors,
  He crosses halls, he goes up-stairs,
He reaches first and second floors,
  Still busied on his own affairs.
None stop him, or a question ask;
None heed the workman at his task.

Despite his cry, Old souls to mend!
  Which into dull expression breaks,
Not moved are they, nor ear they lend
  To him who from old habit speaks.
Yet does the deep and one-toned cry
Send thrills along eternity.

He gads where out-door wretches walk,
   And outcasts under arches creep;
Among them holds his simple talk.
   He lets them hear him in their sleep.
They who his name have still denied,
He lets them see him crucified.

On royal steps he takes a stand
   To light the beauties to the ball:
He holds a lantern in his hand,
   And lets his simple saying fall.
They deem him but some sorry wit
Who serves the Holy Spirit's writ.

They know not souls can rust and rot,
   And deem him while he says his say,
The tipsy watchman who forgot
   To call out, Carriage stops the way!
They know not what it can portend
This mocking cry, Old souls to mend!

While standing on the palace-stone,
   He is in workhouse, brothel, jail;
He is to play and ball-room gone,
   To hear again the beauties rail;
With tender pity to behold
The dead alive in pearls and gold.

In meaning deep, in whispers low
  As bubble bursting on the air,
He lets the solemn warning flow
  Through jewelled ears of creatures fair,
Who while they dance, their paces blend
With his mild words, Old souls to mend!

And when to church their sins they take,
  And bring them back to lunch again,
And fun of empty sermons make,
  He whispers softly in their train;
And sits with them if two or more
Think of a promise made of yore.

Of those who stay behind to sup
  And in remembrance eat the bread,
He leads the conscience to the cup,
  His hands across the table spread.
When contrite hearts before him bend
Glad are his words, Old souls to mend!

The little ones before the font
  He clasps within his arms to bless;
As long ago, so still his wont
  On them to lay peculiar stress.
Besides, of such his kingdom is;
Him they betray not with a kiss.

He goes to hear the vicars preach :
    They do not always know his face,
But him pretend the way to teach,
    And, as one absent, ask his grace.
Nor then his words, Old souls to mend !
Their spirit pierce, or bosom rend.

He goes to see the priests revere
    The image of himself in death :
They do not know that he is there ;
    They do not feel his living breath,
Though to his secret they pretend
With incense sweet old souls to mend.

He goes to hear the grand debate
    That makes his own religion law ;
But him the members, as he sate
    Below the gangway, never saw.
They used his name to serve their end,
And others left old souls to mend.

Before the church-exchange he stands
    Where those who buy and sell him, meet :
He sees his livings changing hands,
    And shakes the dust from off his feet.
Maybe his weary head he bows
While from his side fresh ichor flows.

On mitred peers he turns his face
  Where priests convoked in session plot;
He would remind them of his grace
  But for his now too humble lot,
So his dull cry on ears devout
He murmurs sadly from without.

He goes where judge the law defends,
  And takes the life he can't bestow,
And soul of sinner recommends
  To grace above but not below;
Reserving for a fresh surprise
Whom it shall meet in paradise.

He goes to meeting, where the saint
  Exempts himself from deadly ire,
And in a strain admired and quaint
  Consigns all others to the fire,
While of the damned he mocks the howl,
And on the tinker drops his scowl.

Go here, go there, they cite his word
  While he himself is nigh forgot.
He hears them use the name of Lord,
  He present though they know him not.
Though he be there, they vision lack,
And talk of him behind his back.

Such is the Church and such the State:
　Both set him up and put him down
Below the houses of debate,
　Above the jewels of the crown.
But when Old souls to mend! he says,
They send him off about his ways.

He is the humble, lowly one,
　In coat of rusty velveteen,
Who to his daily work has gone;
　In sleeves of lawn not ever seen.
Nor mitre on his forehead sticks:
His crown is thorny and it pricks.

On it the dews of mercy shine;
　From heaven at dawn of day they fell:
And it he wears by right divine,
　Like earthly kings if truth they tell;
And up to heaven the few to send,
He still cries out, Old souls to mend!

THE WORLD'S EPITAPH.

THE WORLD'S EPITAPH.

I.

ON ART.

WHAT child of art, though genius flash
  Like daylight breaking on his house,
With sunshine can the canvas dash,
  And Nature by the shock arouse?

Burns not in fancy's heaven a sun
  Unsparing of its light's supply,
Whose hues through all emotion run,
  Its landscapes pendant from its sky?

Yet more than this, the child of art
  Can blue and silver light intone:
The order of the stars impart
  To scenes the same as daily shone.

Yet more achieves his graceful wand,
  Adept in Nature's mysteries:
Shining on his creative hand
  The sun sits to him in the skies!

Nor the chill moon his art eludes,
  Orb of the never-blushing ray,
That skims the twilight solitudes
  Out of the reach of busy day.

II.

ON MUSIC.

BEYOND the spheres, dwellers in harmony,
    To whom the instincts of the heart incline,
A silent ocean inundates the sky,
    Choirless the waves, yet not the less divine.
Though suns, the rolling-stock of heaven, may glow,
    As well becomes the bearers of the light,
No other music of the spheres they know
    Save concert in the work of day and night.
Music belongs to man, its empire here:
    It is the living word attuned to love,
And holds the soul of man to be its sphere,
    Though only Heaven can all its rapture move.
When mortals sing the worlds above are mute,
    They gather in the anthem's mingled shout,
They weave the notes, they shape the stringless lute,
    And vibrate softly to the sounds devout.
Then Lyra's constellated embers burn,
    And look below on earth with envious eye
As the soul's echoes to sad music turn,
    And serenade the ear of Deity.

III.

ON POETRY.

Words let the pedagogue dispute
  His logic to express,
Words let the perjurer pollute
  His fortunes to redress.
But winnow from the pearls the chaff of thought,
Lest sense and feeling be too lowly wrought.

Words let the bard to fancy fling
  And at the peril scoff,
Wild thoughts to catch while on the wing,
  The bloom not brushing off.
Then the purblind may look through poet's eyes
And see what things his sight beatifies.

Words in the songster's voice are heard
  And rapture hails the shake,
Words in the orator are fear'd
  While wonder fills his wake.
But when the voice has dropped its tone
Where are the fitful visions gone?

More true the sculptor's marble word,
  The soul is in the cast :
Though but a feeling to record
  It is enough to last.
Strong is the sculptor's marble thought,
To solid life its beauty brought.

Tough is the painter's sunny art
  Which brings the tale to light;
And can the poet not impart
  Such pictures to the sight;
With silent touch the veil remove
That hides the birthplace of his Love?

IV.

ON THE STORM OF LIFE.

THE heaving waters, quarried from the Deep,
  Are piled above in one Atlantine wave.
Indented, lava-washed, the glairy steep
  Hangs doubting o'er its hollow, empty grave.
And now like slimy serpents peak on peak
  Erects its crest to strike the creviced dawn,
Then gnashed in foam before the billows break
  Scatters the barren valley with its spawn.

The World's Epitaph.

Yet fall not, Soul! thy pure and flaky form
   Touched by the briny tumulus were lost.
Better for thee to drift before the storm
   And be along the waste of waters tossed.
No aid accept, no aid to others tend:
Through dusk and foam can only such descend.

Myriads with thee across the darkness driven,
   Snatch at the phantoms howling in the wind,
To share the crash of storms asunder riven,
   And at their lull no further morrow find.
Gust after gust palls on the wretched ear,
   The shriek prolongs the whistle of the gale.
Splash after splash, the graves are coming near,
   One burial flood the surf-encircled vale.
Dark the horizon, lost its gentle line!
   But He who stills the tempest walks the deck.
A like ordeal passed the One divine
   To bear a world in safety through the wreck;
To reef the sails of Night, and through its shrouds
Point out the dawn amid dispersing clouds.

V.

ON THE RAINBOW.

Now spangled Iris springs her shaftless bow
   And with the soul a covenant unrolls.
Poised in the light above, in storms below,
   She opes her book of books, her scroll of scrolls.

Her page, illuminated, spans the sun
   In lines red-lettered after ruby suit,
With symbols round it that in clusters run
   Of interwoven orange, leaves and fruit.

Now shines her golden tunic amber-bright;
   An emerald belt her glossy waist reveals;
And amethyst, divinest of the light,
   About her as a blush of ether steals.

Now faint, and mantled in that orient blue,
   She dies and sinks into the purple shades,
Her mourning vesture fringed with violet hue,
   Which with her in the far horizon fades.

In every shade an emblem of her love,
    Pale be the tint or of the deepest dye :
Saints in her coloured lights are robed above,
    And like the bow illumed by Majesty.

Saints in her coloured lights are robed below
    Where rival banners in their glory rise,
But to the presence all alike shall flow
    Beyond the floral arch of paradise.

EPODE.

The sea-weed proves an easy weather-glass,
    And surging tides an angered moon portend,
Yet will the rapt of earth through whirlwinds pass
    Nor to prophetic signs and tokens bend.

Hear how she reads her storm-drawn scimitar,
    Nought but the splitting up of solar showers,
Yet its untempered blade must point afar
    And give safe escort to the blessèd bowers !

VI.

ON THE SANCTUARY.

To play old ruin on a desert's site
  The rambling stones their chiselled features spread,
And crumbled walls bestow their daily mite
  On sacred earth, the ash-pit of the dead.

Home reared for solitude! the cloister's pride
  Is roofless, jaggèd, ivy-cropped, and lone.
No more the gravestones echo to the stride,
  The day of shrove and feast alike are gone.

Within each chink the lichen guards its hold
  To ripen in the fervour of the moon,
To draw a modest pension from her cold,
  And revel in the fulness of her noon.

The pointed arches let her glory pass,
  Their faded beauty softened in her ray;
The walls see pity in her orbèd glass,
  And hail her as the ghost of ancient day!

The World's Epitaph.

Poised on the moonlit aisle tall columns cast
   Their meaning shadows on the floor of death.
Mute is the chant except along the past,
   Where silent echo holds the courtly breath.

The voice of monks and mitred abbot hushed,
   The table and its waxen lights effaced,
The rich insignia on the altar crushed,
   In heaven is yet their holy record placed.

The crucifix no longer is divine,
   For centuries adored in worship's stead:
Rent are the naked mullions o'er the shrine;
   In dust the painted saint has bowed his head.

The steadfast pines that date religion's birth,
   Set by some abbot once to story known;
That stand apart and measure girth to girth,
   Have now the stature of the earth outgrown.

In straggling waters still the fishes leap
   And low the willow stoops to say its grace,
An hourly service o'er the mouldering heap
   That sanctifies to time the honoured place.

The World's Epitaph.

There is the crystal well; a water-grass
    Stirs into emerald waves the liquid brink;
There thirst the longing lips of lad and lass,
    But never more the living spring to drink.

With arch by buttress stayed the stately bridge
    Spans the fast stream, the stranger of the vale
Whose noise enchants the overhearing ridge,
    Sole minstrelsy within the sacred pale.

Tower, from all towers that bears aloft the palm!
    There better saints poured out a soul of pain,
But now the heavenward chanting of the psalm
    Is silence raining back on earth again.

The truant boy, from overwhelming heights,
    Awe-struck stands gazing at it with dismay:
He clambers down the thicket and alights,
    But dreads the adder's-tongue that guards the way.

The man mature with sadder view admires,
    Catched in the wondrous reverie of the hour.
He gives his living grandeur to the spires,
    And mourns the downfal of religious pow'r.

EPODE.

Hut cracked and crazy, open to the blast
    That whines a dirge, and makes the sick man sad:
By tumbling towers in ruin not surpassed,
    Nor less by slow compassion ivy-clad,
Has it no simple wrong for thee to tell
While the wan abbey works the sleepy spell?

Has he no charm, the poor old man inside?
    To humble ruin close akin he stands,
Though down his wrinkled cheek no moonlight glide,
    Though ivy cling not to his shrivelled hands?
His body wasted, and his senses dead,
The hum of sorrow still runs in his head.

O life monastic, story of the poor,
    The hut holds thy traditionary cells;
The fast is kept alone within the door
    Where self-denial through compulsion dwells.
'Tis there eyes open, and again are closed,
Under the vow by poverty imposed.

VII.

ON NATURE.

CYCLOPEAN shelves from out whose granite base
  Basaltic columns and red porphyry wind,
What volumes rest their lore within thy case;
  What metaphysics of an elder mind!

Of old Silurian times, the rocky age,
  What well-kept registers the changes ring:
But search through every cipher of the page,
  No plague of life the records say or sing.

And thou Devonian era, and the clime
  Where erst the old red waters formed the lands,
The hour-glass set upon a ledge of time
  Has piled upon thy tome its pleasant sands.

Ye too, dark ages of the timber-graves,
  Now tell again how forests, undeplored,
Went in a minute under half the waves,
  And, self-embalmed, for future use were stored.

Then comes the monster-folio, engraved
  On stone, the text of life to illustrate;
To show that no gigantic form was saved,
  By order of a then fastidious fate.

Great Permian epoch, thou whose earthworks tell
  Such rack and ruin of thy middle age,
With what a future does thy volume swell!
  Now ended like unto thy heritage.

Still the deep voices sound upon the beach,
  In waves that tread the golden sands of time,
And to the passing soul a sermon preach
  Interpreted by none, to all sublime.

Nor, high above, the burning lava posed
  With its volcanic torch these shelves shall light
Until by Nature's hand the work is closed:
  Those flames the oldest record of her might.

VIII.

ON TIME.

TIME immemorial, ever-thoughtless dream,
   Failure of all alike from first to last,
That swamps with desolating stream
   The long-enduring Past!
Who the lost tidings of thy day shall tell,
Whose only welcome was to say farewell?

What of thy old endeavour yet survives,
   Told but on stone, shall also drift away:
And so thy reliquary takes and gives
   To lead the foremost minds of man astray!
Better had all that yet escapes from rust
Not ever been, or been restored to dust.

Yet well perhaps thy deep devices fare,
   Since all thy works co-partners with the dead,
May show the anxious mind how vain is care;
   And disabuse the future of its dread;
May warn the hopeful of their scanty lot :
The last to yield, the first to be forgot.

IX.

ON THE FUTURE.

And thou too, Future, sure and slow
    Com'st daily forth anew,
With equal blessings to bestow
    And curses to bestrew;
Thy gifts the half-expired remains
    That breast the passing hour;
Baubles that death awhile disdains
    The later to devour!
Thy wiles acquire thee man's belief,
    The credit of the wise.
Who thinks of thee in time of grief
    Thy promise to despise?
For hope is thine; scarce fledged, she springs
    From out her native east,
Beats off the darkness with her wings,
    And nestles in thy breast.
She mounts on the unrisen orb,
    Breathes its auspicious flame,
Dreams how ere long she may absorb
    The riches of thy name.

Real seems the vision for a day,
  But ere she ends her round
The sun has shed its early ray,
  And autumn holds the ground.
Eclipsed is thence her polar star,
  And distant is her dream;
Not as of late in heaven afar,
  But with receding gleam.
Now from her eyes the scales are cast;
  She throws her glance behind,
And sees her image in the past
  As of another mind!

X.

ON THE SOUL.

FREE as the soul, the spire ascends,
    Heaven lets it in her presence sit;
Yet ever back to earth it tends :
    The tranquil waters echo it.
So falls the future to the past;
So the high soul to earth is cast.

But though the soul thus nobly fails,
    Not long it borders on despair;
It still the fallen glory hails,
    Though lost its conquests in the air.
While truth is yet above, its good
Is measured in the spirit's flood.

Though not its first, its holy light
    Is figured in that mirror's face,
It scarce returns a form less bright
    Than fills above a higher place.
The one was loved though little known,
The other is the spirit's own.

XI.

ON THE SOUL.

SUITOR of Heaven, then take of earth thy fill !
Like languid waters in the path of shades,
Reverse within thy depths the hanging hill,
   Beatify the harsh, the wild cascades.
Look on and listen till thy breath be gone;
Be thou the place, the place be thou, alone.

Stream and its hanging bough in whispers meet
   To gather kisses from the wreaths of foam ;
Clouds find out pools their fleeting forms to greet,
   Or with their shadows over pastures roam.
All join thee in the strolling players' mood,
Soul of the fond, the lone old neighbourhood !

EPODE.

Like smoke arising from its smouldering fires,
    The love of Nature draws up discontent,
And to the gangway of the clouds aspires,
    As if the world to it were banishment.

To triumph and attain all earth can give
    Is proper for the gifted, it is less
Than to the vulgar it may be to live.
    But solitude has not the power to bless.

Then shun the love of glory, save to lift
    A needy world, and give it all the gain!
Set little store on Nature's feathery gift
    Lest falling it shall eddy back amain.

XII.

ON GLORY.

To what new land has Glory gone?
  Her radiance, not less lovely, still invites
The heart on which her presence shone,
  To mingle in her rites.
But now with golden vase her arm outpours
  Along the crimson bank a yellow stream,
And she behind the far horizon low'rs
  To shape the sorcerer's dream.
With tears of light she pledged the mutual vow,
  In dewy lustre robed, at dawn of day;
A guilty hand she only offers now,
  Steeped in the bleeding, ruby-tinctured ray.
A passion of the soul her likeness took,
Only to watch her and to be forsook.

XIII.

ON PEACE.

Peace, let us keep thy natal day!
In us fulfil thy promised way.
Yield to our suit, thy suppliants hear,
O holy being, ever dear!
Be ours in silence, ours in death;
The solace of our parting breath!
Calm passion of the glassy deep,
More than the lull that covers sleep,
More than the still, uncancelled light,
That tints the starry wake of night;
Known best in absence, like the one
So loved when near but most when gone:
Are we to ask of thee no sign,
No vision of thy gift benign,
And by thy memory overcast,
To ply our sorrows in the past?

XIV.

ON THE VALLEY OF THE SHADOW.

THERE comes a breeze, not from the pole,
   Nor from the burning sand;
It comes as if its whiffs had stole
   Across a sunny land;
It has a softness in its dole,
   As if the deep when calm
Had gust on gust with sea-weeds fann'd
   To give it up their balm.

Though Nature's wily voice be glad,
   Playful the curling gale,
And for the asking may be had
   Her most romantic tale,
She sees the heart of man too sad,
   With sorrows overlaid,
To rush again within her pale;
   And triumphs like a maid.

She seeks it in the Cedrus-glades
  At musings to connive;
She stirs the shrinking bough, whose shades
  Seem trodden on alive.
As grief the eye of man pervades
  And makes the lashes wave,
She bids the boughs and breezes strive,
  And earth with sadness pave.

EPODE.

Finds man no rest? Not lofty is his love:
  At most a lunar span above the ground!
Far statelier forms in higher orbits move
  Nor jar on Nature through their silent round,
And act, these strolling monads, longer plays,
Nor utter murmurs louder than their rays.

XV.

ON GENIUS.

THOU one and inextinguishable spark
   That simmerest on the mossy swamp,
Bright though the earth be dark,
   And smothered be the sleeper's lamp :
Genius, thou refuse of divinest light,
   Infatuate fire, self-burning amethyst, .
Whose visage beams when dingy night
   Calls up thy phantom through the mist :
Star of the marsh and fen,
Favoured of Nature, not of men ;
How is thy place below so little known,
With but the quagmire for thine own?

The earth its early course has run :
   No more an infant cradled in the air,
Nursed at the bosom of the sun
   With taintless lips, or thou, O Spirit fair,
Might'st, like thy ever-glorious kin of old,
   Have called it thine to dandle in thy arms !
But now the world is cold,
   Or man is sated with its charms.

It may revive thy claims, may yet impart
The secret of thy choicest art ;
Then, though the stamp of hoofs may mark the mire,
Thou shalt emerge and earth still feed thy fire !

Star of the swamp, thy day the night
   Where heaven vain wealth displays,
And the waste drippings of her light
   Encrust thee round with rays,
Thou shalt adjourn into the dawn,
   With it thy musings blend,
And on the azure of its lawn
   Thy dreamy being end !
Meantime grieve on where Nature grieves ;
Heed not the blessings man achieves.
Thou hast a shout far other lands to hail
When his poor heart has ceased its wail.

To fellow-suffering give an ear,
   In sorrow, thou, and not in glory, trained ;
The spring, exuding ever, dwell'st thou near,
   Where breathless immortality is gained.
Glory within a film of colour glows ;
   The bubble is its wreath ;
But sorrow in an endless river flows,
   Not startled into death.

Cling to thy mire, O Genius bright;
Catch the waste drippings of the light;
Burn 'neath the hoof's unharming tramp;
From the morass renew thy lamp!

The forkèd lustre of the ray unveil,
   And through the dismal swamp thy fetters drag:
A creeping glowworm lingers in thy trail,
   For those set fast within the troubled quag.
Then, yet again the crutchless wanderers save:
   In vain to quit the sedgy waste they strive,
But flounder through a water-venomed grave
   To touch no more its vanished bank alive.
Be it the outlaw asks of thee his way,
The devious torch shall take him not astray:
Fateful thy lot, but mercy in thy gleam,
Fulfil in others thy unfinished dream!

EPODE.

But genius is not sought in every mart:
   One is not wise in lyrics to descant
When once the wit of man rejects his art,
   And warns him coldly to desist from rant.
The pleasant world would thus express its will:
Let science march and poesy stand still.

XVI.

ON DEPARTING PEACE.

STROPHE.

O Peace, why art thou ever on the wing
   With plumes that wave like branches to the sky,
Thy bosom panting out the breeze of spring!
   Make answer, tell me why?

ANTISTROPHE.

To take kind Nature to my fond embrace,
   And share my lot with all,
For this my way I trace.
   By thee repulsed, I disregard thy call.

STROPHE.

And never to restrain thy wayward flight,
   Dear exile from this aching heart opprest?
Wilt thou no more alight
   And set the weary soul of man at rest?

ANTISTROPHE.

I quit the earth and all the cares below,
   But leaving, tap it gently with my wand;
That those who love me, and sustain the blow,
   May follow to the distant land.

STROPHE.

Is not the heart, the stricken heart, thy home?
Bear not thy plumage from it to the skies!
Hither, relenting in thy anger, come,
Nor tear-like float before our longing eyes.

XVII.

ON NATURE.

THOU too, fair Nature, hast thy cloud,
    Peace is not ever thine.
Thy plaintive cry is heard aloud
    As from some holy shrine.
Thy murmurs, rocked upon the gale,
Tell of immortal life a doleful tale.

Thy chant alarms the troubled sky,
    Where late the sun has set,
And the repining heavens reply
    In murmurs of regret.
The prowling sun, though it return,
    Is tangled up in cloud;
Fierce flies the dust as from an urn
    Burst open with its shroud.
The trees bend down to shed their leaves,
Whose drifting circle thee a chaplet weaves.

XVIII.

ON LIFE.

Who would to early life return,
    Recount the days of youth in vain,
The burnt-out fire once more to burn,
    To border on the tomb again?
Once is enough to be a slave;
Once is enough to touch the grave.

A lease of seventy years at most
    Can Nature grant to dust;
The soul is fashioned at her cost,
    And back to darkness thrust.
But, still, the universe is lent
To it while seventy suns are spent.

Meantime the soul attempts to learn
    How Nature first began,
And thence immortal fame to earn
    Within the race of man,
And, Nature's tenure to reverse,
Claims to itself the universe.

XIX.

ON HOPE.

LIKE waters from a sandy well,
   Hope bubbles through the mind :
Her springs to troubled fountains swell,
   Ere scattered in the wind.
The young draw rapture as she flows
And all that dreams afford bestows.

Why, as the waters run away
   Eloping with the hours,
Has every bubble burst in spray?
   So, Hope her own devours!
Thermal her spring in days of old,
Nor now the kindly flow is cold.

But, once fond youth no longer sports
   Save in the vale of years,
Nor with a warmer spring comports
   Than wets the vale of tears.
There when the fount its bubble throws,
The licensed jet through marble flows.

XX.

ON THOUGHT.

Clad in a robe of snow, the Earth
   Proclaims herself a bride;
But scathing blasts and sounds of dearth
   Her nuptial feast deride.
Stripped of the snow her limbs of clay
And wintry breasts lay bared in day.

No bridegroom enters at her gate,
   No handmaids are at hand,
So solitary is her state,
   The festal hour so grand.
Upon the bridal hearth a fire
As from an altar lifts its spire.

One is at hand who feeds the flame,
   And fans it with the hopeless sigh;
While thought consumes without a name,
   Though wedded once to one as high.
But mindful of her brighter days
The thought not faithless with her stays.

Made fast to Nature, as a heart
   That throbs within her depths concealed,
The thought must still subserve its part,
   The sigh, a breath, must be congealed,
And in the inhospitable soil
Be unrequited all their toil.

Once did that thought for Nature live;
   Once did that breath to fame aspire !
Shall not their memory revive,
   Though black the altar, dead the pyre?
Stripped but of their mortality,
Thus offered up they cannot die.

EPODE.

Is not reality the surest friend ?
   Its solid hopes and aspirations please,
And to the mental torment put an end :
   In it alone the world goes at its ease.
Play with the young, their artlessness retain ;
From whence they start a firmer footing gain.
Pass on thy troubles to the curate's care ;
   His profits have their source in man's mischance.
This life is at the best but meagre fare ;
   Let sadness not its poverty enhance.
When death itself salutes thee, look away ;
If it persists, take all it does in play.

XXI.

ON THE SEASONS OF LIFE.

A TREMBLING compass points to age,
   The winter's shortest day;
Four seasons all our heritage;
   Worn-out the beaten way.

Though long the spring-tide, short its hours;
   The years alone are slow;
For joy an endless torrent pours
   Upon the soul below.
And lesser floods bring forth their joys,
Which nothing clogs, and nothing cloys.

A season swelled with many springs,
   A bud-time free from blight,
That flies without the fabled wings
   Which help the angels' flight.
To thee, fair youth, all this is sent,
Pastime scarce changed in changing spent.

The World's Epitaph.

To thee the burning heavens are cool,
    The faded forests green;
The blast that furrows up the pool
    Not to thy senses keen.
To thee the iceberg is a sun
Reflecting days but just begun.

On happy hours thou look'st not back
    As never to return,
Drawn in the meteor's hurried track,
    Thy onward light to burn,
To waste on summer's coming gleam
The fancy of a truant dream.

Nature, to thee scarce human yet!
    The winter in her rear,
Where on the soul the ice must set
    So hard that it will bear!
Where, as the ploughed-up flood congeals
A gelid wind its slumber seals.

Unlike thy days, lascivious Spring,
    That give the bud its scope;
That suns, and showers, and rainbows bring,
    But not as once to hope.
Season of many springs in one
That seemed eternal, and was gone.

EPODE.

Let man through every stage of being wend,
  Like empty barges down the river's slope,
Untimely must his tour of pleasure end—
  With rock and shoal alternately to cope.

Deem life a battle-field as pampas gay,
  Whose hues break lances with the laughing sun:
A game of chess which god and demon play,
  To both of lucky moves an equal run.

XXII.

ON PASSION.

O FAVOURED man, with glance above,
  To thee the heavens are bared;
They hold an atmosphere of love
  By every being shared.
Then is he poor, is he alone
  To whom all heaven is nude?
He lives within a holy zone,
  Though else a solitude.

Friends whom one half the globe divides,
  With seas upon its face,
Feel what a balm between them glides
  To warm the old embrace.
Their newer griefs they still compare;
  Mourn for each other's sake;
Borne down with burdens of self-care,
  Each other's load partake.

But love thus pure scarce feels its might
  The tempest to engage :
An ocean's roll, a meteor's flight,
  The passion in its rage.

Turn to the rapture of the sun,
    And read the lover's dream :
There has the orb in heaven begun
    To wear a redder beam.

A torrid orb is on its way,
    And, kindled in its glow,
Two souls burst into mutual day ;
    Each other's passion know.
Fear holds them back, enchanted fear ;
    Invisible its arm.
A soft impulsion draws them near,
    But impotent its charm.

In sorrow's melancholy stare
    A fever slowly burns,
The eye emits a poisonous glare,
    Its gaze to phrensy turns.
Meantime what clinging hopes sustain
    The lashing of the tides,
And in their tender shells remain
    Unhurt till it subsides!

EPODE.

And is not love a boon to all alike,
  Be it of stranger or of kith and kin?
When fail the clinging roots to burst and strike
  Or draw the nurture to the heart within?

Though man desert, though want the exile face,
  Some tender spirit stands in stead between;
In times of worst disaster and disgrace
  There is a nest yet warm where love has been.

XXIII.

ON THE NUPTIALS.

THRICE-HAPPY, now, in silken cords
   The flowing knot is tied:
A promise in the dream of words
   By scripture sanctified,
The lovers in each other's sight
Feel not as yet the cord drawn tight.

All hearts have burst their icy shell
   And cast it like a skin,
To revel in affection's spell
   And feel to love akin.
Though not for them the torch was brought,
The flame of love a thaw has wrought.

Not to return, that day has shone
   A lifetime to bestow:
Yet how unlike to pleasures gone
   Its yearly ebb and flow!
Balm for all ills that day should prove:
Keep then the wedding gift of love!

EPODE.

The great intent, the beautiful decree
A woman's love, is law divine to thee,
To rule perhaps while wistful eyes express
In full intensity the first caress.
But let the bloom of youth be brushed aside
And slower lips the languid passion guide,
Can she the charm that once encircled her
With power, to fickle man still minister?

XXIV

ON THE SIREN.

Her voice, so clear, in measured time
    Still pours its touching thrill,
Joy of her childhood to her prime
    To modulate its trill.

The song-bird warbles to its mate
    At early burst of spring;
In changeful tune and gurgling prate
    The loving couples sing.

But she whose trembling note so long
    Has echoed love's refrain,
Is moved by no responsive song
    That mingles in the strain.

Yet when her warble fills the air
    All hearts its keeping crave,
And all like song-birds with her pair
    To float on rapture's wave.

Silence returns not as before,
    The echo is not laid ;
The melody that speaks no more
    Within the heart has stay'd.

Oh, not in vain her days have sped,
    Sweet sounds around them throng,
For she to harmony is wed,
    And lives in endless song.

XXV.

ON THE IMAGE.

Once she was seen, and now is seen no more;
    Once was she found, and now is ever lost;
Her beauty known not since, and not before;
    Of all loved forms her image loved the most.

Where is she now? her image tarries here:
    Can two so like, so good, not meet again?
Is one of earth, one of a higher sphere?
    A moment one, and then for ever twain?

Now in conjunction's ever-sweet delight,
    Her beauty vanishing her image left,
One ever moving from the other's sight;
    So happy one, the other so bereft.

She lives, her image else had also slept.
    But is death catching, save as sad and lone?
Alive by her the image was not kept,
    And dead the image is not with her gone.

The World's Epitaph.

EPODE.

All women are alike, though not in type :
All taste the same, at divers seasons ripe.
A first affection, though on record kept,
Falls out of date, is set aside unwept.
No leisure for remorse, the pang postponed,
The unkind parting felt but unatoned.
To this account some penance still is laid,
A debt that to the close is never paid.

A second love this sacrifice requires :
The first to bury ere it quite expires.
A hundredfold the gain for every loss
Should you once more the witches' circle cross.
Still smiles usurp the seat of the caress
    And issue invitations to the lip ;
Still sapid fruits each other's dimples press,
    And courtly flowers each other's nectar sip.

XXVI.

ON THE INFANT AT THE BREAST.

Dot of humanity, thy rosy cheek
    Tints with its flush the breast to which it clings;
Thy lips by industry a living seek,
    And pick up drink at virtue's famous springs.

Nature the store provided for thy gain,
    It else within the frothy well had soured;
Then still thy mother of her goods distrain,
    By thee the font be looted and devoured.

It will convey no poison to thy mind,
    It is thy booty won in honest strife;
No ratsbane with it shall a passage find,
    Churn it between thy lips, it saves thy life.

XXVII.

ON THE WIDOW.

O WIDOW-WOMAN, mourn the dead
    Whom still your homestead needs,
Be crimped the muslin on your head,
    And watered be your weeds.

All else, not only he, is gone;
    Your life lay in his wake.
All will return, though one by one,
    For old acquaintance sake.

A babe its thoughtless prattle brings,
    Nor can it come amiss;
A child to every finger clings
    And asks of you a kiss.

Smile at the little ones who say
    Is father coming back?
Explain his death another day,
    And take another tack.

Ere then how little did you know
    What meant this pilgrimage!
Then own it vain the way to show
    To those of tender age.

All will return, though not apace,
    And God among the rest;
He can supply the husband's place,
    The widow-woman's Guest.

The thoughts of the departed one
    As models still are rife,
And bid you act as he had done
    Ere he gave up his life.

Then all he did was not in vain
    Should you its purpose find;
The words he used will do again
    To speak your inner mind.

EPODE.

The orphans claim her; if a younger dame
She might in time have shared another name.
The world is careless where no harm can come,
But it is partial to the widow's home.
It finds the boy the means to use his head,
And shows the girl how best to earn her bread.

XXVIII.

ON PITY.

From whose estate does pity flow?
  That ever-winding stream,
Too gentle for the scenes below,
  And yet not all a dream!

Though of its healing dew deprived
  The thorny wild grows rank,
The broken reed is soon revived
  That stands upon its bank.

Is it a spring of human love,
  Its way by sorrow worn,
Or flows its bounty from above
  To succour the forlorn?

XXIX.

ON THE BEREAVED.

STROPHE.

Why was this blooming spray entwin'd
    In fresh festoons of grace,
Around this inmost heart to wind
    And all its love embrace?
O that upon my troubled head
    Had come this mighty blow
That numbers her among the dead,
    Thou Author of my woe!

ANTISTROPHE.

Link not another's fate to thine
    Beyond the hour allowed,
Nor in thy troubled heart repine
    Though low by sorrow bowed:
Look only in thy chamber lone
    To emulate the grace
That led her to the heavenly throne,
    The spirit's trysting-place.

The World's Epitaph.

STROPHE.

O that my loaded heart had sunk
  At anchor on her breast;
That both the glacial stream had drunk
  At Nature's poisoned feast;
That both the horn of bitterness
  Had tasted to the lee,
In icy rapture's last caress
  At liberty to flee!

ANTISTROPHE.

Vain man, thy fate to thus upbraid,
  Can it be less than just?
What if thus low thou hadst been laid
  And numbered with the dust!
Hadst thou been fit to take thy place
  Before the judgment-seat,
Who thus devoid of heavenly grace
  These ravings canst repeat?

STROPHE.

O that my body had been cast
  Into the common grave;
Thee, O my soul, thy trial past,
  I had not cared to save!

Can it be justice thus to rend
  The ties of holy love;
Can I to this affliction bend,
  And the harsh will approve?

ANTISTROPHE.

She was in heaven before she died,
  Confess it in thy love.
She in her parting anguish cried:
  I am with Him above!
Then, over her a look of grace
  Stole like a ray of light;
A shadow only crossed thy face,
  Succeeding like the night.

STROPHE.

Was it the will Divine to see
  Her image in the child?
If thus fulfilled be his decree,
  My soul be reconciled!
It was ordained for her to give
  An infant being breath,
To wait and see the helpless live,
  Then sink away in death!

ANTISTROPHE.

Few shun in life a rapid rise,
   An empty rank to gain ;
A vacant place in paradise
   She suffered to obtain !
Thence keeps she watch on this abyss,
   And guards thee with a shield,
Whilst thou art raving at the bliss
   It was not thine to yield.

STROPHE.

O Mother Earth, be desolate,
   All teeming Nature fail,
And hear the orphan's voice narrate
   A father's bitter wail.
To tell, perchance, how the bereaved
   Were taught to bear their lot;
The heart grief-stricken not aggrieved;
   The lone deserted not !

ANTISTROPHE.

In bloody concert fools engage,
   And struggle hand to hand ;
But thou a sadder war shalt wage
   On this unholy strand.

Then on the grave thy gauntlet cast;
    With threats thy Maker greet;
And perish in the trumpet's blast,
    Thy loved no more to meet!

STROPHE.

To take her in my arms and rise
    To scenes of heavenly peace;
To be with her in paradise
    Where human sorrows cease.
To meet my Maker face to face;
    His holy service hear;
And at the fountain of His grace,
    To wash away the tear.

EPODE.

What Heaven has planned, her means have blessed,
Herself takes charge of the distressed;
She for their trial earth began,
Where tribulation is for man.
She, more than all, a mourner loves,
For broken heart her pity moves.
He who best bears affliction's blow
Shall more and more the giver know,
To her resigned his tears shall cease,
And Nature envy him his peace.

XXX.

ON EARLY DEATH.

AGE takes its turn to quit the ground ;
    Its life no further gain :
But why are little children found
    To throng the funeral train ?
Love they the company of years,
Unmindful of their parents' tears ?

Behold their tiny coffins set
    Alongside in the tomb,
As if like twins again they met
    Within a mother's womb.
Bears holiness such scanty fruit
As thus midst sucklings to recruit?

Chilled by the winter's nipping snow
    The rose has cast its flower,
And buds that shoot too late to blow
    Drop with it from the bower.

The starving earth denies a home
To orphans of the world to come.

EPODE.

Some deem it best the young should early die,
    They travel, then, but in advance of fate :
They run away from schools of misery,
    And holidays in heaven anticipate.

XXXI.

ON THE DESERTED.

O LOVELY base-born, earthly child,
  Drop of the olden blood,
Whose glorious soul the virtues wild
  And heathen graces flood;
From the bright roll of Honour's name
No sponsors brave the font to bear thy shame.

O lovely base-born, heavenly girl
  Whose mimic arts the dance inspire,
To be its sad melodious whirl,
  And prompter of its lyre;
Thy feet are holy, not astray;
The world their path, but heaven their way.

O lovely base-born, saintly maid
  Whose voice calls up the sudden tear;
On all alike that penance laid,
  For sanctity is near;
Thy song is sacred as thy love,
Its pathway to the choir above.

The World's Epitaph.

O lovely base-born, lowly one,
    Thy kin in court and camp abide;
Thou trudgest through the earth alone,
    No trappings and no tramp of pride.
They speak in whispers of thy fame,
For it brings blushes on their name.

O lovely base-born, chosen saint,
    Death looks out naked from thine eyes!
They send thee wine now thou art faint;
    They send thee bread that with thee dies.
Thy parted lips in pardon move;
Thy soul departs in perfect love.

Hark! the glad shout, and mighty crush;
    How angels cheering come!
Through miles of holy land they rush
    To bid thee welcome home!
They snatch thee up, in rapture wild
They kiss, they kiss the heavenly child!

XXXII.

ON DISSIPATED YOUTH.

O TIME, to whom the sands a temple raise
To sink as fast as they build up the spire,
The matin and the vesper tell thy praise,
Thou who dost bless all rational desire.

The wise adore thy chimes, the quarter's din,
A melody that to the conscience pleads;
That moves an echo in the ears of sin,
And warns it of the gulf to which it leads.

Earth goes on slowly through the sacred way;
With steps exact it gains the purposed end:
Man stakes eternity to win a day,
Soon to a heavier weight than life to bend.

The young are hastened from their brightest days
To scenes beyond their puny powers to scan,
And led to revel in dead pleasure's ways
That ill befit the riper years of man.

Too soon pale youth plays less than childhood's part:
He scarce can to the bed of sickness creep,
Thence early doomed to take his final start
And poise no more his blooming limbs in sleep.

The heir-presumptive to eternal grace
  Has not an hour of mercy at his claim,
Too late a single mortgage to efface.
  Yet tell not youth that death is taking aim!

The dying look, a spectacle sublime,
  Is still on health restored and pleasure bent.
Shall he not live and mourn thy loss, O Time?
  The sands descend, the vail in twain is rent.

EPODE.

Why not in simple terms describe the school
Where tutors strive to stultify the fool,
To train the germs of self-conceit in grace,
To polish up the faults but none efface;
To foster mockery in place of wit;
To teach false judgment on the world to sit?
Take him to court, give him his golden lace,
His noble birth in all his follies trace;
Take him to church the common prayer to say
And with a lisp the nearest beauty slay;
Then the last supper let him undergo,
Since it is meet to do as others do:
Thence into orgies he shall fondly glide,
And through the sot attain the suicide.

XXXIII.

ON CONSCIENCE.

HARSH is the crown thy brow around,
  Thou hapless beggar's child !
Why is thy head with prickles bound?
  To make thy name revil'd ?
Thy voice shall whisper why in vain,
  So feeble is its force :
Can stony heart its beat regain
  And melt into remorse?

Pass on, poor child ; for thy name's sake
  Leave this infected place,
Lest soon thy peace of mind partake
  The qualms it would efface.
Nor in the crowd attempt a breach,
  Though more than warrior bold ;
But to the babe thy lessons teach
  Before it is too old.

XXXIV.

ON SLUMBER.

The lamp goes out, the eyelids close:
  Are angels then at hand
To guard the spirit in repose,
  And at the pillow stand;
With curtained wing the watch to keep,
And cast a shadow over sleep?

Is thence the wicked one less bold
  Who seeks his prey by night?
His eyes, to love and pity cold,
  Fear they the angels' light?

The peace of conscience, with its smile,
  Works it on man a charm
To keep the spirit safe from wile,
  But not the soul from harm?
To hold the sleep in their embrace,
Is this the guardian angel's grace?

XXXV.

ON THE PILLOW OF THE WRETCHED.

WEARY of life, in mind deprest,
  The eyelids droop but crave in vain;
The thinking part denies them rest,
  For it must cling to pain.
The griefs of old as waters come
  That gather in a brook;
The thinking part has there no home,
  By every ripple shook.
How like a dream! and yet no sleep
  Assigns to it a resting-place;
It has a course that it must keep:
  The pillow shares the race.

EPODE.

The wide affections which a world assail,
Not man's vocation be it to bewail!
Weep for a sister, for a brother grieve,
A child bemoan, for time is a reprieve.

Regret a neighbour even as a friend,
In silence mourn a parent to the end.
Lament a benefactor, oft deplore
The early friend whom thou canst see no more.
But, though the losses quickly may betide,
Be prompt the mental conflict to decide.
Divert the thoughts into a lively strain;
To dwell too long on trouble turns the brain.

XXXVI.

ON A MOTHER.

THE soul must not repine !
 Not when a parent, perhaps the last
In old affection's line
 Shall bear away the past?
She who once left us not a day,
 And now is loth to close her sight
On those who yet may stay
 To fill the void with sorrow day and night?

The eye no more shall weep !
 Not for a mother, though she wept
Beside us in our sleep,
 And ghostly vigil kept
When Sickness in pale garments lay
 Upon the pillow at our head
To mark her quiet way
 Between us and the dead?

Not shed a tear to soothe the brain,
 Not yield the heavy sob?
The inward agony restrain,
 Despite the bursting throb?

Her dear and silent lips not press,
  Not kneel by her again;
Not utter in our last distress
  A prayer that she remain?

Let then the wounded spirit heal
  Ere it has time to smart;
Let law the memory repeal
  When those we love depart;
Then may the heart its load defy,
  And with no muffled beat
Strike up the note of victory
  At Nature's great defeat.

EPODE.

Whether the son be doomed to stay
  A mother's parting words to hear,
Or by unlooked-for, sad delay
  She stops his obsequies to bear;
The mourner yet to themes shall wake
In which no sorrow need partake.

Nature confirms in all the right
  To dissipate the cloudy past,
Lest when a blossom falls its blight
  The ills of death on others cast.
Not all is lost while power divine
Allows the day again to shine.

From human depths must suffering rise,
   Till it a burnt-out ember leave,
Then shall its former peace surprise
   The home where old affections cleave:
Then sleep the reddened eyes shall bind,
And force the tears to lag behind.

So love itself, not lost to thought,
   Its clinging is constrained to cease,
And, not through vain repinings sought,
   Is with the past ere long at peace.
Then with the dead, in memory blest,
The heart shall be at perfect rest.

EPODE.

How beautiful is laughter's ring,
   It is the spirit's bell;
The siren's witching strain can bring
   No such ecstatic swell,
The harp's delirious cord can fling
   No such assuring spell.
Let not the ears to sorrow cling
   The spirit's single knell;
Let not the hands each other wring
   To bid the long farewell.

XXXVII.

ON THE OUTCAST.

O MISERY, whose sorry way
   All steps must tread at last,
Thy part alone how many play,
   With thee their portion cast:
From morn to night on the check-mated board
Theirs the lost game, its teachings theirs to hoard.

And well may such the doubt address
   Why they were put to life for only pain,
Their infant features modelled to express
   What others act for gain!
But, pledged the pleasant world and all its charms,
No place to them remained except thy arms.

The refuse of the sunny breeze
   Thou gatherest for thy poor;
The cutting hail in gusts that freeze
   Their limbs outside the door.
Heaven's roof lets in the rain and wind,
Where then can they a shelter find?

Ask Heaven to bid the famine cease,
  With plenty at her beck;
Ask her to lend a hand to ease
  The millstone round the neck;
Relentless, she no help to such can tend
Whose shaking limbs in worship never bend!

They laugh, but penury the more
  Is on their pointed cheek;
They sleep, and golden visions score:
  The windfalls of the weak.
They, waking, clutch them in their hold,
But with the dream departs the gold.

Their sleep the riot of the dead
  Whose sins deny them rest;
A world with terror overspread,
  The soul by hell-hounds prest,
The wave of dream heaves up and down,
The floating sense in lava-floods to drown.

Now to the rotten, herbless bank
  They drift and strike the shoal;
The stream is thick, the sedge is lank;
  It is the common goal.
All thence afresh their start shall take
To run for the eternal stake.

EPODE.

The city of the poor, by fancy built,
    Stands on the mind that such a scene unfolds :
Though growing wealth draws poverty and guilt,
    Suffering so massed no faithful eye beholds.
To labour is a right, to beg a wrong ;
    They both are freely at the choice of all ;
The sick and lame to their own mansions throng ;
    The public purse is open to their call.

XXXVIII.

ON CHARITY.

CHARITY, thou whose maiden name
    Was never changed for mortal love,
Now as of old who art the same,
    To sorrow's home the holy dove;
Is all thy beauty dim and worn,
Veiled since the hour when woe was born?

Charity, who with unshut ear
    Hast tended at the cripple's door,
Thou art content to ask and bear
    The one-toned story of the poor!
Still the same tale, so often told,
Creeps to thy bosom from the cold.

Art thou perchance the long-lost star
    Not fallen but immortal still,
Which missed and mourned by all afar
    Art here with souls who suffer ill?
Charity, hast thou left yon sphere
To do the work of pity here?

EPODE.

What, murmur still and still devoutly strain
The feeling element from pain to pain?
If charity began at home, how few
Were called upon its tributes to renew!

XXXIX.

ON THE SAINT.

SAINT, now in paths of light,
  Let drop awhile thy newly grafted wings,
And, in the dead of night,
  Devote a leisure hour to earthly things;
Bear witness, once, how ill thy fellows thrive
In haunts thou didst not visit when alive.

Champions to hunger trained, these scenes engage;
  The boards unlicensed, unapproved the play:
One look of sorrow on the blackened stage
  Would break upon it like the invading day,
Would show to thee how low is laid the plot,
And from what depths is tragedy begot!

Invest with memory the lyric verse
  Whose accents stun the air;
The menace and the look rehearse;
  And laugh the loud despair!
Fail not the thought and gesture to acquire,
Then light up heaven itself with tragic fire!

Yes, on thy way to bliss,
   Mimic these graceless acts before the blessed :
Repeat the howl of hunger, and the hiss ;
   Perform a benefit for the distressed !
Then shall kind eyes be turned to earth below,
And, on the wretched, looks like thine bestow.

EPODE.

Is pity all in all ; whose then the hand
That speeds its almoners by sea and land ?

XL.

ON THE SISTER OF MERCY.

Of those whose turn comes round to weep
   Shall Pity shed the tear;
The drip puts weary grief to sleep
   Though no relief be near.

The kindred soul of thoughtless days,
   To pleasure only known,
The word of sympathy delays
   For sorrow not its own.

But she a stranger at the gate
   Where none besides attend,
Asks leave to see the desolate
   And enters as a friend.

XLI.

ON THE STATESMAN.

Ruler of men, for whom the place
    Of forethought was devised,
Thy noble destiny embrace,
    For honour thou hast prized!
Thou, thy loved country's willing hack,
    Wouldst lift this earthly dome!
The world itself is on thy back,
    The weight of every home.

Thy share of life is not its joys;
    Thou dreadest their excess:
Thine is a task which half alloys
    The round of happiness.
Thy presence is the Future's page;
    Between our hour and thine
The world has run another stage,
    To prosper or decline.

Yet from the annals of the dead
    Are thy forewarnings brought;
Historic lore is daily bread
    To thy prophetic thought.

The else neglected paths maintained
    By signals on the road,
The gateway to thy rest is gained
    Under the heavy load.
Thus travelling sweetly to thy sleep,
    As once to study's grove,
Dreams not untrue thy senses steep
    In man's immortal love.

EPODE.

'Tis thus the young draw profit from the old :
Their works inherit, mines of wealth untold !

XLII.

ON OLD AGE.

The young despise the old;
   To them wise saws are as a musty book;
A wisdom dead and cold,
   A marble urn and nook.

The old despise the dead
   Whose fading memory they put away,
Among the tomes shelved never to be read,
   Up to the dying day.

The old, do they despise
   The last view through the avenue of strife;
The setting to the rise;
   The backward view of life?

EPODE.

The natural laws are sworn upon the sun;
   The lips that spoke them kissed the sacred orb;
But man's long story only has a run
   That nobler fictions may its thread absorb.

XLIII.

ON PENITENCE.

IF second sight could look askance
  And with the morrow chime,
If second thought could steal a glance
  Into the book of time,
Thou, O repentance, second pain,
Hadst lived not hourly to complain.

Repentance more than second pain,
  So many times recast;
Corrected and revised again,
  The last time not the last!
So would the feeble will of man
Its thread resume where life began.

O vain regret, the yester-pang
  That festers in the mind;
The rankling and envenomed fang
  That envy leaves behind;
Seek not the days for ever gone;
Recal not deeds to be undone!

For thee, vexed soul, by early fate
    The fond regret was meant,
To warn the conscience, when too late,
    Its errors to repent.
Then stay the wheel, insert the spoke,
The project of the past revoke!

O after thought, with siren's voice
    The conscience cease to fret,
Whispering to it thy second choice,
    Step-mother of regret!
She, O how well we know is nigh
Who pastures on the human sigh!

Repentance, second pain, what hour
    Escapes thy web of grief,
What sense of fate eludes thy pow'r,
    Though firm in its belief?
By thee the scarry soul is rent,
And life through life made penitent.

Had we not done what we had done,
    The crown had been attained;
Had we but pleasure let alone
    The glory had been gained!
So in the past the timepiece beats:
And what has struck, its strike repeats.

No shade its fostering light can blind
  While summer yet is here,
But dark the desert is behind;
  Another hemisphere;
A side apart for penance set
To dwell on thee, O vain regret.

XLIV.

ON MADNESS.

Now, torch of reason, dark and fierce thy fire!
    Thy ruby flambeau thickens in the sight;
An angel wields it in his touching ire,
    And drops its molten tears along his light.
In no disguise he puts on horror's shape,
    And like the moon he rises in the night
Beyond the sun's asylum to escape;
    While birds of prey are silenced in his flight;
Courier too dread their instincts to mislead,
He who pursues a spirit to the dead.

Is she of woman who in gentler moods
    Now melancholy saps for past excess?
Is she of man, who tiger-like now broods,
    And is a mourner at her own distress?
For vain it is that drooping head to cheer,
    That cheek of dull affection to caress.
There hangs upon the eye a sullen fear
    Which proffered love not only fails to bless,
But wakes the dreadful look that seeks to know
Why heaven is sinking into depths below!

The World's Epitaph.

Behold a second angel true to all,
   Welcome to her, the harbinger of change!
He comes the clouds of anger to recal;
   The wondering sense from madness to estrange.
O lest the blinking sun its curtain drop,
   And the bright interval once more derange,
The refluent reason and affection stop!
   For death the dregs of memory exchange,
That she the house of mockery may spurn,
And in a lucid hour to God return.

XLV.

ON DESPAIR.

The moon is up, a haze is in the air,
    Dull looks the way to all beyond the spot;
No eye can scale the mist to regions fair,
    Though oft beyond has flight of fancy shot.
The mind is up, but hazy is the brain;
    Its choked-up passion lingers at its source,
Hope stretches out her wings with obvious pain,
    And knows scarce whither to direct her course.
The sun, the vaulting stars, are wondrous bright,
    But not the path of mortals to disclose;
The spirit strives to rush into the light,
    But feels the tomb its burden interpose.

XLVI.

ON THE STRUGGLE FOR IMMORTALITY.

PERTURBED, storm-ridden Uranus! how far
　Art thou from those who look to thee for rest,
And in the track of elemental war
　Would trench the heavens thy stronghold to invest!
Though many try, not facile is the task;
Slow the progression to the good they ask.

The wish and thought, man's double star, allured
　Into a common circle rise and fall,
To glory's clime and trial not inured;
　Yet would they take the one deep plunge of all!
To spirits orbit-bound, hard is the way
Through gusty shadows to the unknown day.

EPODE.

Faith walks by night, she, safest guide of all,
The great somnambulist, can never fall!
She dreams her way, and constant in her rise
Wakes up to find herself in paradise.

XLVII.

ON MAN.

What is the earth to thee, thy heaven of yore,
   Poor vessel of its breath?
It can sustain thy soul no more,
   And gives thee up to death.
Undying youth the lot that Nature drew,
Be thou content her beauty to renew.

Earth still may be thy hiding-place,
   To have and hold in peace;
Thou mayst complete the tour of space,
   Though thy frail being cease.
The ages but await their own;
Thou to their dawn shalt be a thing unknown.

Yes, beauteous, ever fair is Nature's fate;
   Untutored and uncurbed is her controul;
She bids thee be the witness of her state,
   And sops thy wondering spirit in her soul;
She sports with thee in the competing game,
To be in turn her glory and her shame.

The World's Epitaph.

She loves in thy discourse to laugh and weep,
   In all she prompts an equal part to bear,
Thy fasts and festivals alike to keep
   To speed an old, to greet a coming year.
True to the moment, false to all beyond
Her pledge she only gives to break the bond.

Beware her winning ways, resistless wiles;
   She charms the heart that it may better yield:
She who can mourn the dead while she enfiles
   The youth of nations on the bloody field !
She sets a crown upon the victor's head,
While vultures scream the service of the dead.

Repel her when with thine her counsel chimes;
   Heaven for a nobler destiny beseech ;
Be armed religion-wise against her crimes
   Taught thee in whispers sweet as woman's speech.
Be not in hands like hers the feeble sport:
She grants no passports to a higher court.

XLVIII.

ON FATE.

One moving power the world pervades,
    To good and evil blind:
It elevates and it degrades
    Its shadow called the mind.
A hidden power, that now impels
    The martyr to his crown,
Now in the base assassin dwells
    To strike his brother down.

Fate who alone this system plann'd
    Has yet herself outbid:
Unconscious her all-mighty hand
    In which the power she hid.
To selfless glory ever tends
    Her impulse to create,
While in her likeness man ascends
    To consciousness of fate.

Owl-like midst highest destinies
    Is she seen far away,
With film before her stony eyes
    Which nictates night and day

The World's Epitaph.

A film so dense, that it conceals
   All deity behind.
She nothing to herself reveals;
   Her love and justice blind.

Her realms man looks on in her stead,
   But in the bold survise
His vision forfeits to the dead :
   A self-borne sacrifice.

XLIX.

ON DESPOTISM.

Not those who thirst can drink the despot's blood;
   Too many crave, 'twere little to divide.
His days are numbered for some secret good;
   Their term can Providence alone decide.
At her own time, and free of our controul,
She from the body shall pluck out the soul.

L.

ON PRIDE.

Say not all pride is false! the most beloved
    Are those who scorn their spirit to repress,
Their hearts not less by kindred pity moved
    Amid the world's distress.

Perchance the knave may cross his way
    With canting, easy prate;
May not the proud keep him at bay,
    Nor care how much he hate?

Pride is a shield by wisdom's hand
    With social law engraved;
With emblems ever pure and grand
    From elder epochs saved.

Pride is a shield of whose defence
    All virtue claims the right;
Pride is a shield without pretence
    For all who nobly fight:

The honoured who resist the lie,
And turn it from their door;
The strong who for the weaker die;
The rich who serve the poor.

LI.

ON THE PRISONER.

O PRISONER in thy cell,
  Thy roving meditations yet uncurbed,
Why, like a saint in hell,
  Is thy lone soul perturbed?
Hast thou been wronged by all outside thy grate?
  Why care they not,
But stand below the arch to laugh and prate;
  Thyself by all forgot.

O prisoner, law be thine;
  And it can hang or set thy virtue free.
Then why repine?
  Heed not the chances, all abandon thee.
O prisoner, in thy cell,
  Cease thus to commune with thyself alone;
Thou art a saint in hell;
  Thou art some holy one!

Mind not thy virtue, it may be;
  But mount the scaffold nobly, look above;
Thus set thy virtue free,
  And give thy carcass up to human love.

LII.

ON REMORSE.

Unholy ghost, in thee remorse
    Acts leisurely its part;
By steady unremitting force
    It makes thee what thou art.
The coil of life shall it unwind,
    The days it has to last;
Let loose the torments of the mind,
    And bind them to the past.
The hour of death, the hour of doom,
    These from thy presence flit;
No morrow's thought can break the gloom
    Where sharp remorse has bit.

Shallow the crime thy heart decreed,
    And easy to embark;
But to thy eyes, that saw the deed,
    Inscrutable and dark.

Thy hand, which set the blood to flow,
  Did not a moment wince :
Thy hand which aimed the cruel blow
  Has struck it ever since.
Thy soul no novel pang can brand ;
  No other threads thy sight :
Scarce hell itself is seen at hand
  A passage to invite.

LIII.

ON HYPOCRISY.

Emblem of guilt, ensconced within
  The margin of thy crimes,
Who thy memorial, steeped in sin,
  Hast spelled a thousand times;
Who when the last dark line is read
  Beginn'st the page again;
Who, still, when the last pang hath sped,
  Art on the track of pain;
Behind those laboured looks of good
  A clouded conscience hides,
Though it besmears the hands with blood
  That dangle at thy sides!
Although the crime on conscience press,
  To this thou are inured;
But sore the brand of guiltlessness,
  Henceforth to be endured!
Hast thou no service for thy voice
  Except the truth to spurn;
Is there no being of thy choice
  On whom thy heart to turn?

The self-preached sermon of the cell
  Has voices still and clear;
Canst thou not force the horrid spell,
  And trust another ear?
Truth is the vizor of the good;
  And scorching to thy sight;
Why dost thou wear its polished hood,
  And brave its racking blight?

EPODE.

In prison, Church and State go hand in hand;
  Chaplains for truth, and advocates for lies:
These cleanse the sinner, these the sinner brand,
  So lost between the two the captive dies.

LIV.

ON THE MASK.

Here temples cheer the solitude,
    There overlap the haunts of weal ;
Here are the tenants wild and rude,
    There in the ermine of their zeal.
Yet join thou in the stirring rite,
Nor mark the saintly hypocrite.

Wouldst thou condemn his mellow face
    Or sort the hidden signs within,
And not discern a mark of grace
    Among the spots upon his skin?
Is such a form of worship done
To meet the eye of man alone?

Pious thyself, and so he deems,
    Approve another's saintly make ;
All that thou seem'st to be he seems ;
    Applaud him for thy honour's sake.
His hood thy mask, his mask thy hood,
Ye are the same in flesh and blood.

LV.

ON SELF-RIGHTEOUSNESS.

Who shuffles, cuts, and deals the cards of grace,
   Who plays at faith, hope, charity, to win?
Who, not of poor and self-debasing race,
   Sits at the ladder's summit safe from sin?
How comes it he forgets the rule of Three;
   Counts not its losses, and its winnings grave,
The holy, blessed, and glorious Trinity!
   To play with it is not the soul to save.
What if with him a game of chance it play,
And shape its rule by what the Scriptures say?

LVI.

ON CUNNING.

Pray on, poor idiot, preach thy bill of fare,
   With gaping mouth and hollow moan!
Thine eyes have cunning in their stare;
   Thy voice the beggar's groan.
Can it be true that grace divine
Sits on a soul so false as thine?

For, idiot, in thy grace attired,
   Thy features speak it not,
As if, with all thou hadst acquired,
   Thy visage were forgot.
Eyes with a stealth that wins a bet,
Lips to a form of worship set.

LVII.

ON BELIEF.

O REASONABLE soul, thy range
    Else checked by bounds of clay,
Who but desires his place to change
    For some celestial way?
Say in what hopes, what fears to die;
    What unction to receive:
Faith, poor must be thy ministry,
    To think what men believe!

The classic regions sink below,
    There heroes meet again
In lofty pride and converse slow;
    A hell devoid of pain.
In paradise by genius scored
    Upon the starry chart,
The intellect is still adored,
    And art still worships art.

Between two worlds, the last but one,
    Of hell and heaven the mean,
The leper's soul is kept alone
    Till he for heaven is clean.
The grave forgot, that home of old
    Nor front nor aft a door;
The velvet turf by ages roll'd;
    The garden of the poor!

EPODE.

Mind not the ancients, they are dead at best,
    Be it beneath us, midway, or above;
Mind not the moderns, such as are at rest;
    But give the living races all the love.

Turn to the heathen with a softening care;
    Call him to join the small and chosen sect;
His soul for more than common news prepare;
    Mid lurid warnings name him thy elect.

LVIII.

ON THE DEATH-BED OF THE WISE.

RESPECT the death-bed of the wise,
  Count not their coming end, in quiet past,
The prelude to a sad surprise,
  The soul in torments cast.

Thou art a saint as often told
  From thy dear lips; and thou art sure
The crown of holiness to hold;
  The birthright of the pure.

Yet deem not those who see outside
  The limits of thy sphere,
Unfit thy profits to divide
  In heaven, as well as here.

If all their work be sin, forgive;
  They toiled for thy estate;
They smoothed the way for thee to live;
  Such was their happy fate.

Long since with Heaven they signed a peace :
  The treaty neither broke ;
Nor shall its obligations cease,
  For neither can revoke.

LIX.

ON THE PHILOSOPHER.

Thou genius of the stars whose glass
   Points to the fields on high,
To gauge the glories as they pass,
   Remote, yet looking nigh;
Know'st thou that living thus in light,
Thy way is dark, thy soul is night?

The gleams of thy arched palace throw
   A shadow in thy way;
Gleams that from a Creator flow,
   Yet blind thee to his day.
Philosophy, though born above,
Curdles the milky-way of love.

O genius, sin no more, but pray;
   A whirlwind marks thy place,
The stars to scatter in dismay,
   And hurl thee into space.
Not thus thy thirst for lore assuage:
Is it not sin the heavens to gauge?

LX.

ON DELIRIUM.

Before thy time is up, by warnings scared,
   Worse than the landlord's call to quit or pay,
Thou, puzzled soul, shouldst hold thyself prepared
   To leave the body; soon is judgment-day.

Not yet immortal, no from mortal clove,
   Be like the virgin wise with lamp in hand;
Put on thy lightest garment for thy move,
   Thy passport ready for a better land.

Life is a dream, be death no less a dream;
   'Tis meet that thou who seek'st a better sort
Shouldst flash thy magic lantern up the stream,
   And with the slides of paradise disport.

The spirits give thee concerts in the air;
   Lute-strings and voices mimic rapture's strain!
Though not a sound and not a figure fair
   May be outside the circle of thy brain.

The World's Epitaph.

Yet to thy vision those translucid arms
  And loving chords invite, they bid thee come.
Before, not harmony's united charms
  Could run thee up the gamut to thy home.

The pallid cloud, a cumulus divine,
  Draws on thy footrise to its step of gold;
To other eyes it may or may not shine;
  To thee its signs of bliss are manifold.

And though a mild delirium only wakes
  This blest finale of a rental day,
O what a happy turn thy phrensy takes
  For thee, poor soul, ejected from the clay.

Life is no truer dream, then shall not death
  The dream of dreams ascend its leaden sky?
It has a strange reality beneath,
  Has it above no like reality?

LXI.

ON THE CLOSE OF LIFE.

BE it the world as many deem
　　Should founder in the past,
Or, as to many more may seem,
　　Is in a frame to last,
There is an hour that comes to all
When sun must cease to rise and fall.

The pulse of thought must stop its beat
　　At Nature's bright array,
The look of thought must cease to greet
　　The bursting of the day.
That evening fades or morning shines,
The glazing eye no more divines.

Whose the blank night that crowds the dome
　　When mortal strives for breath;
Whose the blank day which in that home
　　Lights up the face of death,
A day whose lovely sunrise wreaks
Its glory on the heart it breaks!

EPODE.

O candid spirit who look'st on below
At human nature with a pitying love,
Unto all blame imparting sorrow's glow,
   Which the shrill note that mocks thee cannot move;
Thy message is divine, its trembling voice
   With thee inclines us longer to converse.
High-born, immortal being of our choice,
   While with regret we gather to disperse,
Our ringing ears still listen to thy chant,
   Its words escort us to one common bourn,
In us the long-enduring lesson plant,
   And at thy coming silence bid us mourn.

LXII.

ON THE CHURCHYARD.

OLD dormitory, last of parish bounds,
    How men come sleeping here, with shutters closed,
To add a remnant to the other mounds,
    Those cast-up sums, in line on line disposed.

On happy Sunday when the moving crowd,
    To show thee flush of life, turns out of church,
Who but amid the old discerns a shroud,
    As if the maw of death had made a lurch?

Wondrous thy threshold they can dare to cross,
    Mined as it is, and into tunnels scraped;
Its every quake to human life a loss,
    Its every step a spot where it has gaped.

Yet, such the confidence that use begets,
    Men set their dwellings on volcanic soil,
Nor once a thought of death or danger frets,
    Oft as the flames below their pyre uncoil.

The World's Epitaph.

If there prevails in men a wholesome dread
   To walk, however lightly, on the grave,
Lest it disturb the slumbers of the dead;
   Far worse a danger to themselves why brave?

Why fail they to recal that every place
   Is mined by busy worms at work beneath?
Though they be safe at the volcano's base,
   Let all who tread the churchyard count on death.

LXIII.

ON THE TOMBS.

Here mother Earth sepultured lies,
  Here with the buried sleeps.
But whence the crop of effigies
  Which from her quarry creeps?

Turned into stone are the elect;
  They muse beside the walk,
Like living orators erect;
  But never more to talk.

The honoured name to memory dear
  An epitaph reveals;
In more than mourner's heart could bear
  The sharp-cut letter deals.

The yew-tree's sad deploring mass
  Droops like surviving grief,
Whether it grows upon the grass,
  Or on the bas-relief.

LXIV.

ON DEATH.

O SPECTRE, waning form of man,
    Frail image of his sleep;
Now stony is the nostril's span;
    The spirit's ancient keep.

So too those cheeks of sallow hue,
    Veined by the marble's dye;
So too those lips of pallid blue
    That chime mortality.

On a dead sea recumbent lies
    Thy figure, as a wave:
Afloat are now the open eyes,
    Turned upward from the grave.

That one last look on heaven remains,
    Her equal in its peace;
Not as of late when aches and pains
    Were working thy decease.

And now in terror lies thy skill,
  All shrinking from thy sight;
The reptile's touch imparts a thrill
  Less deadly in its blight.

No sympathy adorns thy face;
  No horror of the tomb;
A stoic heart to thus erase
  All knowledge of its doom.

LXV.

ON THE RESURGAM.

I SHALL arise in Thee, O God,
  And claim Thee from the dust;
I shall arise and bless the sod
  That proves Thee more than just!
What, O my soul, thou lonely one,
  Refuse thy only friend,
Whose presence at thy birth had shone,
  Who watched thee to thy end?
I shall arise and look for Thee,
  O Saviour of the race!
What, O my soul refuse to be
  A chosen heir of grace;
Thou who hadst else to dust returned
  And famished in the tomb;
Thou whom the universe had spurned
  Despite the Virgin's womb?

> I shall arise, and with my breath
>   The Holy Ghost receive!
> What, O my soul, prefer thy death
>   To this divine reprieve?

THE END.

LONDON:
PRINTED BY C. WHITING, BEAUFORT HOUSE, DUKE STREET,
LINCOLN'S-INN-FIELDS.

www.ingramcontent.com/pod-product-compliance
Lightning Source LLC
Chambersburg PA
CBHW031332230426
43670CB00006B/322